D1393605

Mary Berry

ABSOLUTE
FAVOURITES

Mary Berry

ABSOLUTE

FAVOURITES

1 2 3 4 5 6 7 8 9 10

BBC Books, an imprint of Ebury Publishing
20 Vauxhall Bridge Road,
London SW1V 2SA

BBC Books is part of the Penguin Random House group of companies
whose addresses can be found at global.penguinrandomhouse.com

Penguin
Random House
UK

Copyright © **Mary Berry 2015**
Photography by **Georgia Glynn Smith**

Mary Berry has asserted her right to be identified as the author of this
Work in accordance with the Copyright, Designs and Patents Act 1988

This book is published to accompany the television series entitled
Mary Berry's Absolute Favourites, first broadcast on BBC Two in 2015.
Mary Berry's Absolute Favourites is a Shine TV production.

Executive Producers: **David Ambler** and **Karen Ross**
Series Director: **Ed St Giles**
Production Manager: **Dan Bankover**
Production Co-ordinator: **Annie Boutle**

First published by BBC Books in 2015

www.eburypublishing.co.uk

A CIP catalogue record for this book is available from the British Library

Editorial Director: **Lizzy Gray**
Project Editor: **Kate Fox**
Copyeditor: **Kate Parker**
Food Stylists: **Georgia May, Lisa Harrison, Lizzie Kamenetzky**
Prop Stylist: **Liz Belton**
Design: **Lucy Gowans**
Production: **Helen Everson**

ISBN 9781785941832

Printed and bound in China by C&C Offset Co., Ltd

Penguin Random House is committed to a sustainable future for our
business, our readers and our planet. This book is made from Forest
Stewardship Council® certified paper.

CONTENTS

INTRODUCTION

IT HAS BEEN SO REWARDING assembling the recipes for this book as I've been able to bring together some absolute favourites, past and present – not just my own favourite dishes but ones that have gone down particularly well with friends and family over the years.

While it's lovely to experiment and try out new things, you shouldn't feel obliged to serve something different to your guests each time, especially if they're people you don't see regularly. There may be certain dishes that you love doing and that are always devoured with enthusiasm by your guests – so if they have praised a dish, why not serve it again, particularly if it's one that you enjoy making and can produce with a confident flourish? Just as you might go to a well-loved restaurant expecting to be able to order your favourite food, so your guests might look forward to being served something they've enjoyed before. They might even be disappointed if you don't produce your signature dish!

The recipes here come into that category; they're all tried-and-tested crowd pleasers. My own favourites change over time – I'm constantly finding new ones to add to my repertoire or playing around with the ingredients of an old recipe to give it a fresh twist. The Mini Beef Wellingtons (page 28), for instance, are a take on the full-scale version of the recipe but much lighter and crisper, perfect for serving as nibbles at a drinks party, while the Smoked Haddock Risotto (page 146), topped with poached rather than hard-boiled eggs, is a delicious variation on the more familiar kedgeree.

We have access to such a wealth of different ingredients nowadays, making it so easy to ring the changes. When I first started cooking, the only greens that were available apart from cabbage and sprouts were peas and French or runner beans. When it came to lettuces there was the basic round Dutch lettuce or London, also known as Cos or romaine. Now you can buy mangetout and sugar snap peas, tenderstem broccoli and fennel, and every type of lettuce imaginable, not to mention tomatoes, peppers and even carrots in extraordinary rainbow hues. Chilli peppers are everywhere now, too –

particularly favoured by the young. I love all the new arrivals and try to incorporate them in my dishes alongside the old favourites.

Wherever possible, I also like to use home-grown or locally produced ingredients. I've always had a strong interest in how food is produced and in knowing where it comes from. At home when I was a child, Dad produced much of our own food. He kept pigs – I can remember him cutting up the carcasses on our kitchen table and my mother using the meat to make sausages. She kept hens, too, so we'd have fresh eggs, while my father grew all our vegetables, including masses of celery, which I can remember bundled up in newspaper with the green fronds poking out of the top. Like my parents, my husband Paul and I also grow much of what we eat: fruit as well as vegetables, and lots of fresh herbs – including parsley, dill, basil, mint and tarragon, a real favourite – which I use all the time in my cooking for their vibrant flavour. I almost never use dried herbs.

I find these days that people are increasingly interested in how their food is sourced, preferring to buy items that are locally grown or sustainably farmed. The television series that accompanies this book is all about where our food comes from, and I've had a lovely time exploring different locations – from catching prawns on the coast and fly-fishing in the River Test to seeing how Stilton and mozzarella are made. Farmers' markets have really come to the fore now, too, and I visit them at every opportunity. Seasonal produce can be so much cheaper than in the supermarket, and I so enjoy chatting to the actual producers, hearing them talk with real passion about the things they make and grow. Allotments have become increasingly popular, too, helping us all to get away from the idea that food has to be perfectly shaped and without a blemish – a crooked carrot or misshapen apple tastes just as good, often more so if carefully cultivated. I've got into the habit of cooking with whatever's in season and, if there's a glut of something – plums or other soft fruit from the garden, for instance – I just pop what I don't immediately use in the freezer to have to hand another day.

While I've always loved food, I didn't fall in love with cooking until I started domestic science classes at school, where I discovered I had a natural talent for it and was hugely encouraged by my domestic science teacher, Miss Date. This has made me conscious of how important it is to pass on cooking skills to the next generation and to acquire an interest in food preparation from a young age. I used to cook with my children and so enjoy cooking with my grandchildren. With each session I like to focus on a new skill, and I watch as they carry out the recipe step by step, perhaps baking a cake or cooking something for supper – the boys had particular fun preparing Saturday Night Pasta (page 198), a perfect one-pot dish for a family meal.

All-in-one dishes must be among my favourite types to cook. I'm very much in favour of using the oven as much as possible – for casseroles, roasts and other one-pot meals – rather than the hob, where dishes need much more attention to ensure that they don't dry out or burn on the bottom of the pan. This collection is full of one-pot dishes, from the Harissa Spiced Lamb with Cannellini Beans (page 84) to the Roasted Sausage and Potato Supper (page 62) – just so easy to put together and a real winner with both family and guests. As well as avoiding mountains of washing-up, these sorts of dishes are perfect for informal entertaining, I find, especially when we all tend to dine in the kitchen these days.

They are also part of my general mantra of preparing as much as you can in advance. Forward preparation really helps, I believe, enabling you to relax so much more with your guests. Also, you never know what might happen on the day, especially if you're running a busy household. With this in mind, I've given 'Prepare Ahead' tips in almost every recipe, suggesting how the whole dish or elements of it may be prepared in advance so that only the minimum needs to be done before serving. Even for dishes that you cook at the last minute, such as the Prawn and Ginger Noodle Stir-fry (page 138), you can cut up the vegetables well beforehand or mix the ingredients for the sauce so that it's all ready to add to the pan.

Wherever possible I've also indicated where a recipe is suitable for freezing. It's just so useful having a few dishes ready in the freezer – such as meatballs (page 70) or fishcakes (page 143), which can be wrapped individually and taken out as you need them. Sausages are useful to have ready-frozen, too, and a few chicken or pheasant breasts, carefully wrapped, which can be defrosted and pan-cooked in very little time.

This philosophy applies throughout the book. In 'Canapés & First Courses', for instance, I've gathered together a selection of sure-fire favourites that are either very simple to prepare or easy to make in advance. For a starter nothing could be simpler than the Gravadlax with Mustard and Dill Sauce (page 34), for instance, dead easy to

put together and yet it never fails to impress. If you are feeling more adventurous, why not try my Mushroom Mini Scotch Eggs (page 24) as a canapé, made using quail's eggs and with the advantage of being fully vegetarian. Yes, they do take time and care to make – but they're absolutely worth it!

I've included two chapters on ways to cook meat and poultry, each offering a broad selection of favourite dishes for any occasion, from ever-popular burgers and cottage pie (pages 77 and 78) to more formal offerings such as Turkey Crown with Orange (page 122) and Canon of Lamb with Mint Gravy (page 90). While vegetables, rice and pasta have chapters of their own, you'll find one or two meat dishes tucked away in these sections, including a speedy way to make lasagne (page 201) and a delicious quiche (page 168).

With fewer fishmongers around today, you may find that the fish counter at your local supermarket offers the best source of fresh fish and seafood. I've devoted a separate chapter to fish along with a number of recipes using prawns or shrimps, which must be one of nature's convenience foods as they're so quick to cook, not to mention a personal favourite of mine. If you're a fan of seafood, then the Seafood Linguine with Fresh Tomato Sauce (page 202) is another winner, full of flavour and very healthy too, while paella (page 207) never fails to please.

Vegetarian cooking has entered the mainstream and the chapter on vegetables includes a selection of delicious main dishes, some to be served warm, such as the Onion, Courgette and Blue Cheese Puff Tarts (page 173), and some cold, including the Superfoods Salad (page 158) and Asian Slaw (page 183) – each super-healthy and designed to be made ahead. Among the side dishes a really trusty standby must be the Red Cabbage (page 185), which goes so well with game and duck and can even be frozen.

For anyone with a sweet tooth no meal is complete without a pudding and I've included a tried and trusted selection here, too, often variations on a classic theme, such as the Mini Apple and Almond Cakes (page 248), which are based on a favourite recipe for apple cake, or the luscious Banoffee Meringue Roulade (page 245). When you're preparing a dinner party cold desserts are definitely the best option. They can be very simple – you often don't want anything too heavy at the end of a meal, in any case – such as the Fast Gooseberry Fool (page 237) or even homemade ice cream (page 226), which you could make up into a Raspberry Knickerbocker Glory (page 233) – spectacular-looking yet so easy to assemble at the last minute, and a real treat.

There are lots of sweet treats to choose from in the 'Tea Time' chapter, including several new takes on old favourites, such as my assistant Lucy's Strawberry Slices (page 267), which provide an irresistible twist on the standard Victoria sandwich. Some of the recipes in this section would work equally well as puddings, too, in particular the Lime and Polenta Cake (page 285), delicious served warm with a dollop of crème fraîche. Meanwhile, children will enjoy making the biscuits and little iced buns (pages 264 and 270). Wrapped in cellophane and with a handwritten label, they make a lovely gift.

In addition to the recipes themselves, you'll find practical tips scattered throughout the book. In 'Cook's Notes' (page 292) I've jotted down various points to bear in mind when using the recipes. I've also included conversion tables (page 296) and a few notes on basic serving quantities and store-cupboard ingredients that you might find helpful (page 295). All the dishes shown on the television series appear in this book, along with many more that it wasn't possible to show – I can recommend every one of them to you. I do hope you'll enjoy trying them and, in the process, discover a few absolute favourites of your own.

Mary Berry

Canapés &
First Courses

THE TRICK WITH CANAPÉS AND FIRST COURSES is to choose something that will both delight the eye and tempt the tastebuds but without you having to assemble too much at the last minute when you should be mingling with your guests. It's with this in mind that I've gathered together here a selection of recipes that really fit the bill for any occasion, from a more formal drinks party to a meal with friends and family.

When you're serving canapés, it's best to restrict the selection to only three or four so that they stand out and can be really savoured by your guests. I always include dips among these, to be served with a selection of vegetable crudités, and the Two Quick Dips here (page 19) would be ideal for this purpose. You could put these together with the Devils on Horseback (page 30), for instance, and the Scrambled Egg and Bacon Tartlets (page 26). The ready-made croustade cases that I've used for these are a real godsend when it comes to preparing dainty nibbles for a drinks party. They make it so simple to put these together, while looking as though you've gone to a lot of effort!

When asparagus is in season, nothing could be nicer as a first course – either served on its own with a little butter or hollandaise sauce (page 44) or mixed with other ingredients and made into an elegant salad, such as the Tomato, Mozzarella and Asparagus Salad with Basil Dressing (page 40). For the dressing, I've suggested using shop-bought fresh pesto, easily available from supermarkets if you don't have time to make your own. I've also incorporated it in my Cheesy Cheese Spirals (page 20), which are ideal for preparing ahead as they can be frozen, if need be, and reheated in a trice.

My chief tip for selecting a first course is to go for one that can be made up and placed ready on the table before your guests sit down, allowing you to concentrate instead on guiding people to their places and filling their glasses. The Smoked Trout, Avocado and Tomato Tians (page 50) or Goat's Cheese and Shallot Tarts (page 23) are the perfect dish for a dinner-party starter as they both look impressive and can be prepared well in advance.

Soup is ideal for colder days, but because it's difficult to keep warm, I'd reserve it for a meal with a few friends rather than a large formal gathering. I've included three of my favourites here: Creamy Asparagus (page 37), Tomato and Basil (page 38) and Wholesome Bean (page 39) – any of which could be served on their own for lunch with some good bread on the side.

TWO QUICK DIPS SERVES 6

THESE TWO DIPS REALLY COMPLEMENT EACH OTHER and are great for a party to serve with bread sticks, tortillas, crisps or vegetable crudités.

SOURED CREAM AND HERB DIP

PREPARE AHEAD
This dip can be kept, covered, in the fridge for up to 3 days.

300ml (10fl oz) soured cream
2 tbsp chopped parsley
2 tbsp chopped mint
2 tbsp chopped basil
1 garlic clove, crushed
1 tbsp lemon juice
salt and freshly ground
    black pepper

1 Measure everything into a bowl, season well with salt and pepper and mix to combine.

2 Cover with cling film and chill in the fridge for a minimum of 2 hours for the flavours to combine and develop. The longer you leave the dip, the stronger it will taste.

AVOCADO GUACAMOLE WITH TOMATO AND CHILLI

PREPARE AHEAD
This dip can be made up to 4 hours ahead.

2 ripe avocados, peeled and stoned
2 large spring onions, finely chopped
2 large tomatoes, quartered,
    deseeded and finely chopped
1 small red chilli, deseeded and
    finely chopped
juice of 1 lime (see tip on page 72)
1 garlic clove, crushed
salt and freshly ground black pepper

1 Roughly chop the avocado into tiny pieces, tip into a bowl and stir so that the pieces break up and squidge together. Add the remaining ingredients, mix well and season with salt and pepper.

2 Cover with cling film and chill in the fridge for at least 30 minutes for the flavours to develop. It will keep for a day in the fridge, but will discolour if left too long.

CHEESY CHEESE SPIRALS

THESE WILL BE EVERYONE'S FAVOURITE CANAPÉ, young children included. With their light texture and intense cheesiness, they'll just vanish from the plate! I have used a whole packet of puff pastry here so it makes plenty, but halve the recipe if you wish to make fewer.

MAKES 128 SPIRALS
(64 OF EACH KIND)

PREPARE AHEAD
The uncooked rolled squares can be kept for 1–2 days in the fridge. Once cooked, the spirals can be stored in an airtight container for 1–2 days and reheated to serve.

FREEZE
Freeze the cooked spirals and reheat for 10 minutes at 180°C/160°C fan/ Gas 4. The uncooked rolls can also be frozen. Defrost in the fridge and cook as in step 5.

1 x 320g packet of ready-rolled, all-butter puff pastry
plain flour, for dusting
2 tbsp fresh red or green basil pesto
2 tbsp Dijon mustard
75g (3oz) mature Cheddar cheese, grated
75g (3oz) Parmesan cheese, grated
paprika, for sprinkling
1 egg, beaten
salt and freshly ground black pepper

1 Preheat the oven to 220°C/200°C fan/Gas 7. Line two baking sheets with baking paper.

2 Unroll the pastry and lay on a floured work surface (or see tip). Roll out a little thinner, to form a square measuring about 36cm (14in) on each side. Using a sharp knife, cut the pastry in half. Spread the pesto over one half and the mustard over the other, making sure to spread right to the edge of the pastry. Scatter the cheeses over each half and season with salt and pepper, then sprinkle the mustard side with paprika.

3 Slice each half in half again widthways and divide each into four squares, so that you have 16 squares in total, each measuring 9cm (3½in).

4 Roll up each square tightly to make a sausage shape, brushing the last strip of pastry with the beaten egg mixture so that the roll stays stuck down. Wrap in cling film and chill in the fridge for 10 minutes. Unwrap and slice each roll into eight discs. Use a serrated knife to carefully saw through the pastry and avoid squashing the discs.

5 Lay the discs flat on the baking sheets, spaced slightly apart, and bake for 10 minutes or until puffed up, golden and crisp. Serve hot or warm.

TIPS
Roll out the pastry on a piece of cling film to stop it from sticking to the work surface. You can use the cling film to help roll up the squares, rolling it up with the pastry to make a tight sausage shape.

Don't forget to egg wash the last strip of pastry on each square, so the spirals do not unroll during cooking.

GOAT'S CHEESE AND SHALLOT TARTS WITH WALNUT PASTRY

IDEAL FOR A FIRST COURSE, served with some dressed salad leaves, these are also great for a picnic or light lunch. Take them to the seaside to enjoy as you sit on the beach. You'll need the goat's cheese in a tub, which is soft and spreadable, rather than the kind in a roll.

MAKES 8 TARTS

PREPARE AHEAD
Once cooked, these will keep for up to 2 days in the fridge.

FREEZE
The cooked tarts can be frozen. Defrost thoroughly at room temperature before serving – the texture of the goat's cheese topping may suffer if defrosted quickly.

FOR THE PASTRY
175g (6oz) plain flour, plus extra for dusting
100g (4oz) cold butter, cubed
1 egg, beaten
30g (1oz) walnuts, roughly chopped
salt and freshly ground black pepper

FOR THE FILLING
1 tbsp oil
500g (1lb 2oz) banana shallots, thinly sliced
2 tbsp balsamic vinegar
1 tbsp light muscovado sugar
300g (11oz) soft goat's cheese
2 eggs, beaten
2 tbsp chopped parsley, to garnish

1 You will need two four-hole Yorkshire pudding tins. Preheat the oven to 200°C/180°C fan/Gas 6, and slide a large baking sheet into the oven to get hot.

2 To make the pastry, first measure the flour, butter and a little salt into a food processor and whizz until the mixture resembles breadcrumbs (or place in a mixing bowl and rub the butter into the flour with your fingertips). Add the beaten egg and 1 tablespoon of water and mix until a ball of dough is formed.

3 Roll out the dough thinly, on a floured work surface, to about 3mm (⅛in) thick, then sprinkle the chopped walnuts over the pastry. Cover with a piece of cling film and roll over the cling film to press the nuts into the pastry. Cut out eight large circles using a pastry cutter or saucer as a guide and use to line the Yorkshire pudding tins. Place in the fridge to chill while you make the filling.

4 Heat the oil in a frying pan, add the shallots and cook over a high heat for 2 minutes, stirring frequently. Lower the heat, cover with a lid and cook for 10 minutes until soft. Add the vinegar and sugar and cook for about 15 minutes, stirring every now and then, until dark brown and caramelised. Set aside to cool.

5 Put the goat's cheese, beaten eggs and 1 tablespoon of the parsley in a bowl, season with salt and pepper and mix until smooth.

6 Prick the base of the chilled tart cases all over with a fork, then spoon the shallot mixture into the pastry cases, dividing it evenly between the two tins. Pour the goat's cheese mixture over the shallot mixture, again dividing it equally between the tins.

7 Slide the tins on to the hot baking sheet and cook for about 20 minutes until the pastry is crisp and the filling just set and golden. Sprinkle with the chopped parsley and serve warm or cold.

MUSHROOM MINI SCOTCH EGGS

PANKO BREADCRUMBS are a variety of dried breadcrumbs used in Japanese cooking but widely available here in the UK. They give a crisp, light-textured finish that is perfect for these little Scotch eggs. These can be cooked ahead and reheated quickly in a lightly buttered frying pan to crisp them up.

MAKES 12 EGGS, OR 24 CANAPÉS

PREPARE AHEAD
These can be made and fried up to 12 hours ahead. The mushroom mixture can be made up to a day in advance and kept in the fridge until you are ready to coat the quail's eggs.

12 quail's eggs
4–6 tbsp plain flour, for coating
1 egg
75g (3oz) panko breadcrumbs
about 4 tbsp sunflower oil
celery salt, to serve

FOR THE COATING
a knob of butter
2 banana shallots, very finely chopped
250g (9oz) chestnut mushrooms, finely chopped
30g (1oz) panko breadcrumbs
1 egg, beaten
salt and freshly ground black pepper

1 To make the mushroom coating, first melt the butter in a frying pan. Add the shallots and fry over a medium heat for 10 minutes until soft, then add the mushrooms and fry for a further minute. Cover the pan with a lid and allow to steam for 2 minutes, then remove the lid and fry over a high heat until browned and the liquid has evaporated. Season with salt and pepper, add the breadcrumbs, then stir everything together and leave to cool. Stir in the beaten egg and mix well.

2 Put the quail's eggs in a pan of cold water and bring to the boil. Cover with a lid and boil for 1½ minutes, then drain and leave to cool in very cold water (see tip on page 120). Peel the cooled eggs and set aside.

3 Sprinkle the flour on to a plate, beat the egg in a shallow bowl and spread the panko breadcrumbs on another plate. Roll the eggs in the flour and then, using your hands, coat each egg in the mushroom mixture so that it is completely covered. (This is best done with damp hands to stop the mixture sticking to your fingers.) Roll the balls in the flour, then dip in the beaten egg. Roll the balls in the panko breadcrumbs and chill in the fridge for 30 minutes to firm up.

4 Heat the oil in a frying pan (see tip), add the balls and fry over a high heat for 4–5 minutes until golden and crisp, turning carefully with a fork and spoon as each side browns. You may need to do this in batches so as not to overcrowd the pan. Transfer to kitchen paper and side aside to cool slightly.

5 To serve as canapés, slice each Scotch egg in half and season the yolk with celery salt before serving, ideally while still warm.

TIP
To test that the oil is hot enough, drop in a pinch of the breadcrumb coating. If it sizzles immediately, then the oil is hot enough to start cooking the Scotch eggs.

Scrambled egg and bacon tartlets

THESE ARE RIGHT UP MY STREET! Using ready-cooked croustade cases, heated through until they are crisp and golden, helps cut down on preparation time. These are best made and eaten immediately, still warm, while the croustades are lovely and crisp.

MAKES 24 TARTLETS

1 packet of 24 ready-made
  croustade cases
3 rashers of smoked back bacon
5 large eggs
15g (½ oz) butter
1½ tbsp full-fat crème fraîche
1 tbsp snipped chives
salt and freshly ground black pepper

1 Heat the croustades in the oven according to the packet instructions. While they are heating, fry or grill the bacon on both sides until crispy, then snip into small pieces with a pair of scissors. Place in the oven to keep warm with the croustades.

2 Beat the eggs and season well with salt and pepper. Melt the butter in a pan, cook the eggs over a medium heat until just scrambled, stirring frequently and taking care not to overcook them as they should be soft. Stir in the crème fraîche and most of the chives.

3 Spoon the eggs into the warm croustades and scatter the crispy bacon and reserved chives on top. Dust each with a grinding of black pepper and serve warm.

TIP
If serving at a party, to avoid having to assemble the tartlets from scratch just as your guests arc arriving, the bacon can be prepared in advance and the chives snipped. Then just scramble the eggs and assemble at the last minute.

Mini beef Wellingtons

A TAKE ON FULL-SIZED BEEF WELLINGTON and just as much of a treat, these are perfect for a special occasion. For these delicate tartlets I've used filo instead of puff pastry and lined them with a little horseradish sauce for added kick.

MAKES 24 TARTLETS

PREPARE AHEAD
The tartlet cases can be made up to a day ahead, to fill on the day.

2 x 25cm (10in) square sheets of filo pastry
butter, melted, for brushing
125g (4½oz) tail beef fillet
1 tsp runny honey
1 tbsp oil
4 tbsp hot creamed horseradish sauce
salt and freshly ground black pepper
1 tbsp chopped parsley, to garnish

1 You will need a 24-hole mini muffin tin or two 12-hole ones. Preheat the oven to 200°C/180°C fan/Gas 6.

2 Brush each sheet of filo pastry with melted butter and lay them side by side. Cut each sheet into 25 squares, each measuring about 5cm (2in). Take two squares. Place the first square, butter side down, into one of the moulds of the muffin tin. Place the second square on top at an angle to the first one to form a star shape, and press down. Repeat with the remaining squares (with two left over), placing them in the remaining holes to make 24 mini tartlet cases.

3 Bake in the oven for 5–10 minutes until golden and crisp. Remove from the oven and transfer the tartlet cases to a baking sheet to cool completely.

4 Slice the fillet steak into 1.5cm (⅝in) cubes, season with salt and pepper and toss in the honey. Heat a frying pan until it is very hot, add the oil and fry the steak on all sides over a very high heat for a couple of minutes until golden (but still pink in the middle). Transfer to a plate to rest for a minute or two.

5 Divide the horseradish between the cooled pastry cases, sit one warm piece of fillet inside each tartlet and sprinkle with the parsley to serve.

DEVILS ON HORSEBACK

AN OLD CLASSIC BUT ONE I LOVE and have not put in a book for years! These are ideal for preparing ahead and cooking just before your guests arrive. You can cook them in the oven or grill, though the grill gives a slightly crisper result.

MAKES 24 ROLLS

PREPARE AHEAD
These can be prepared in advance and kept in the fridge for up to 2 days, cooking to serve.

12 rashers of very thin, smoked streaky bacon (see tip)
12 soft-dried pitted prunes

1 Preheat the oven to 220°C/200°C fan/Gas 7 or the grill to medium-high.

2 Cut each rasher of bacon in half widthways. Slice each prune lengthways into two and wrap each half tightly with a piece of bacon.

3 Place on a baking tray and roast in the oven for about 10 minutes, turning halfway through – or cook under the grill for 2–4 minutes on each side – until the bacon is crisp. Serve warm.

TIP
If very thin bacon is not available, you can stretch each rasher with the back of a knife.

PLATTER OF CONTINENTAL MEATS WITH SALSA AND DIP

THIS SELECTION OF BOUGHT, DRY-CURED MEATS, offset by a clean-tasting fresh salsa or a creamy horseradish dip, is perfect for sharing as a starter. The salsa benefits from being made in advance as this helps the flavours to develop. Serve the platter with slices of crusty bread.

SERVES 6

PREPARE AHEAD
The salsa and horseradish dip can both be made in advance and stored in the fridge – the salsa (covered) for 2–3 days and the dip (kept in a container) for 1–2 days. They can be assembled with the meats 2–3 hours before serving and kept covered.

75g (3oz) sliced pastrami (about 8 slices)
75g (3oz) sliced salami (about 10 slices)
75g (3oz) sliced Parma ham (about 7 slices)
100g (4oz) rocket
25g (1oz) Parmesan cheese, shaved
75g (3oz) black olives, in oil, drained

FOR THE SALSA
½ cantaloupe melon, peeled, deseeded and finely diced (about 150g/5oz prepared weight)
1 small mango, finely diced (about 150g/5oz prepared weight)
1 tiny red chilli, deseeded and finely chopped
3 tbsp olive oil
juice of 1 lime (see tip on page 72)
salt and freshly ground black pepper

FOR THE DIP
200ml (7fl oz) tub of half-fat crème fraîche
3 tbsp hot creamed horseradish sauce
1 tbsp chopped parsley

1 To make the salsa, mix all the ingredients together in a small bowl and season with salt and pepper.

2 To make the horseradish dip, mix all the ingredients together in a small bowl and season with salt and pepper.

3 Arrange your selection of cooked meats on a large, flat serving platter and scatter the rocket leaves, Parmesan shavings, and a few of the olives on top. Serve with the remaining olives, salsa and horseradish dip in small bowls on the side.

GRAVADLAX WITH MUSTARD AND DILL SAUCE

THIS IS MY ALL-TIME FAVOURITE dish for serving as a first course. It needs to be made at least 24 hours ahead, but I keep it in the freezer already cured so it is there when I need it. Salmon fillet cut from the middle of the fish is best for this dish as the meat is the most tender and full of flavour.

SERVES 6–8

PREPARE AHEAD
After curing and brushing off the salt, the salmon can be stored, wrapped, in the fridge for up to 1 week. It can be sliced ready for serving then covered and chilled in advance on the day. The sauce can be made 1 day ahead and kept in the fridge, or it can be made without the cream 1 week ahead, the cream folded in on the day.

FREEZE
The salmon can be frozen but not the sauce as it will curdle on thawing. Part defrost the fish to make it easier to slice.

600g (1lb 5oz) middle-cut salmon fillet, skin on
2 tbsp dried dill
2 tbsp coarse sea salt
1 tsp freshly ground black pepper
2 tbsp caster sugar

FOR THE SAUCE
2 level tbsp caster sugar
2 level tbsp Dijon mustard
1 tbsp white wine vinegar
75ml (3fl oz) sunflower oil
75ml (3fl oz) double cream, softly whipped
2 tbsp chopped dill
salt and freshly ground black pepper

TO GARNISH
dill sprigs
lemon wedges

1 Arrange a large piece of foil in a roasting tin. Sit the salmon, skin side down, on the foil. Sprinkle over the dill, salt, pepper and sugar, pressing these down into the fish, so the top of the salmon is completely covered. Bring the foil around the fish to make a parcel, sealing all the open edges. Put another tin or tray on top and weight it with tins or scale weights so the salmon is pressed down. Transfer to the fridge and leave to cure for 24 hours.

2 To make the mustard and dill sauce, first place the sugar, mustard and vinegar in a bowl and season with salt and pepper. Whisking by hand, gradually pour in the oil, continuing to whisk until thickened. Fold in the whipped cream and dill.

3 Remove the weights and the foil from the salmon. The meat should be dark pink, with most of the curing ingredients, but not the dill, dissolved into it. Dab off any grains of salt that remain and pour away any excess liquid around the fish.

4 To serve, cut into wafer-thin slices 2–3mm (⅛in) thick and at an angle of about 45 degrees, cutting the flesh away from the skin. Allow 4–6 slices per person, the quantity depending on the thickness of the slices. Garnish with dill sprigs and lemon wedges and serve with brown or crusty bread and the sauce.

CREAMY ASPARAGUS SOUP

EXACTLY AS IT SAYS IN THE TITLE: nothing clever, just delicious fresh soup. This is perfect for using up asparagus stalks if the tips are being incorporated in another recipe; in which case, just garnish with some chopped fresh chives instead of the asparagus tips.

SERVES 6

PREPARE AHEAD
The soup can be stored in the fridge for up to 12 hours and then reheated, with the asparagus tips cooked and added just before serving.

FREEZE
This can be frozen, without the asparagus tips, for up to 1 month.

25g (1oz) butter
1 onion, finely chopped
350g (12oz) floury potatoes (such as King Edward), peeled and cut into small cubes
2 large bunches of asparagus (about 500g/1lb 2oz)
900ml (1½ pints) chicken or vegetable stock
150ml (5fl oz) double cream, plus extra to serve
salt and freshly ground black pepper

1 Melt the butter in a large saucepan. Add the onion and potatoes and fry, stirring frequently, over a medium heat for about 5 minutes or until the onion has started to soften.

2 Trim the asparagus by snapping off the woody end of each spear where it breaks naturally. Remove the top two inches of each tip and set aside, then chop the stem into short lengths.

3 Pour the stock into the saucepan, bring to the boil, stirring, and boil for 8–10 minutes or until the potatoes are cooked. Add the chopped asparagus stems, cover with a lid and simmer for another 8 minutes or until tender but still bright green. Season with salt and pepper.

4 Whizz until smooth in a food processor or using a hand blender, then pass the mixture through a sieve and return to the pan.

5 Cook the reserved asparagus tips in boiling water for 3 minutes and drain.

6 Heat up the soup and check the seasoning, then stir in the cream and pour into individual bowls, garnishing each one with a swirl of cream and three asparagus tips arranged on top.

TOMATO AND BASIL SOUP

FULL OF VIBRANT FLAVOUR, and so healthy too, this must be my favourite soup.

SERVES 6

PREPARE AHEAD
This can be stored in the fridge in a sealed container for up to 2 days.

FREEZE
The cooled soup can be poured into a freezer-proof container and frozen for about 1 month. Defrost overnight in the fridge or at room temperature for 4–6 hours.

2 tbsp oil
1 large onion, roughly chopped
1 large carrot, finely chopped
2 celery sticks, sliced
2 garlic cloves, crushed
2 x 400g tins of chopped tomatoes
750ml (1 pint 6fl oz) vegetable or chicken stock
3 tbsp tomato purée
1 tbsp light muscovado sugar
2 tbsp chopped basil
salt and freshly ground black pepper

1 Heat the oil in a large, heavy-based saucepan. Add the onion, carrot and celery and fry over a medium heat, stirring continuously, for about 5 minutes or until nearly soft. Add the garlic and fry for a further minute.

2 Add all the remaining ingredients except the basil and stir to combine. Bring to the boil and season with salt and pepper, then lower the heat, cover with a lid and simmer for about 15 minutes or until the vegetables are all tender. Tip in half the basil and check the seasoning.

3 Whizz until smooth in a food processor or using a hand blender, then return to the pan to reheat. Serve piping hot and garnished with the rest of the chopped basil.

WHOLESOME BEAN SOUP

A VERY HEALTHY, HEARTY SOUP, perfect for winter days. Bean soup mix is readily available from the supermarket, but if you are unable to buy it, use a 100g (4oz) combination of beans, pulses and pearl barley instead. Whatever mixture you choose, you'll need to soak the dried beans overnight before making this soup. It's best not to season the beans before boiling, as salt can toughen their skins.

SERVES 6–8

PREPARE AHEAD
The soup can be made up to 2 days ahead and stored in a sealed container in the fridge.

100g (4oz) bean soup mix, soaked in cold water overnight following the packet instructions
1 tbsp olive oil
a knob of butter
2 garlic cloves, crushed
2 onions, chopped
2 celery sticks, finely diced
2 medium carrots, finely diced
2 litres (3½ pints) strong-flavoured vegetable stock
1 bay leaf
1 sprig of rosemary
2 x 400g tins of chopped tomatoes
2 tbsp sun-dried tomato paste
2 tsp caster sugar
salt and freshly ground black pepper
2 tbsp chopped parsley, to garnish

1 Drain the soaked beans and rinse in cold water, then set aside.

2 Heat the oil and butter into a large, deep saucepan. Add the garlic, onions, celery and carrots and fry over a high heat for 5 minutes. Lower the heat, cover with a lid and cook gently for about 10 minutes, stirring occasionally.

3 Add the stock, bay leaf, rosemary and drained beans and bring to the boil, stirring. Boil for 10 minutes, then add the tomatoes, tomato paste and sugar. Stir to combine, bring back up to the boil, then reduce the heat and simmer, uncovered, for 50 minutes to 1 hour until the beans and vegetables are tender.

4 Remove the bay leaf and the rosemary sprig, season with salt and pepper and serve garnished with chopped parsley.

Tomato, mozzarella and asparagus salad with basil dressing

THIS SALAD IS ALL ABOUT THE FLAVOUR of the ingredients, hence it is best made with ripe tomatoes and when locally grown asparagus is in season. It would make a substantial starter or light lunch. Also pictured overleaf.

SERVES 6

PREPARE AHEAD
The salad can be assembled 2–3 hours before serving and kept in the fridge – bring up to room temperature before eating. The dressing can be made 1–2 days in advance and stored in the fridge.

20–30 asparagus spears (about 500g/1lb 2oz), woody ends snapped off
6 medium, ripe tomatoes
1 large bunch of basil, shredded
about 75g (3oz) rocket
300g (11oz) mozzarella pearls, each broken in half
salt and freshly ground black pepper

FOR THE DRESSING
1½ tbsp white wine vinegar
1 tsp Dijon mustard
3 tbsp olive oil
2 tbsp fresh green basil pesto (see tip)
1 tsp caster sugar

1 Cook the asparagus spears in boiling, salted water for 3–4 minutes until tender and bright green in colour, then drain and refresh in cold running water until cooled.

2 Thinly slice each tomato and arrange in a neat line down one side of an individual plate, scatter with the shredded basil and season with pepper.

3 Arrange 3–5 asparagus spears (the quantity will depend on size) in a criss-cross pattern over the tomato slices. Pile a small handful of rocket leaves next to the asparagus and sit some of the mozzarella halves on top. Season with salt and pepper and repeat for the five remaining plates.

4 To make the dressing, mix all the ingredients together and whisk in a bowl to combine (see tip), seasoning with salt and pepper. Drizzle over the rocket and mozzarella and a little on the asparagus. Serve at room temperature with rye bread or bread rolls.

TIPS
Most supermarkets now sell fresh pesto in the chiller cabinet. It tends to be less salty than the variety sold in jars, with a superior colour and flavour, but, being fresh, it has a much shorter shelf life. However, it can be frozen and used within 1 month.

Use a clean, screw-top jar to make the dressing. It makes it easy to shake the ingredients together to mix, and the dressing can then be stored in the jar in the fridge.

EGGS AND BROCCOLI ROYALE

THIS IS A TAKE ON ASPARAGUS ROYALE, the broccoli making a delicious alternative. Be sure to use the tenderstem rather than the standard kind as it's much more delicate and dainty. The hollandaise sauce is very simple to make and gives a lovely smooth result that doesn't curdle as long as you keep stirring.

SERVES 6

PREPARE AHEAD
The eggs can be cooked in advance, plunged into chilled water to stop them cooking and stored in the fridge. Reheat briefly in a pan of boiling water, off the heat, for about 20 seconds to ensure that the yolk stays runny. The hollandaise can be made 1–2 hours earlier and kept warm in a wide-necked vacuum flask. The broccoli can be cooked up to 6 hours ahead, refreshed in cold water and reheated for a minute in boiling water to serve.

450g (1lb) tenderstem broccoli, trimmed
6 large eggs

FOR THE SAUCE
2 tsp lemon juice
2 tsp white wine vinegar
2 large egg yolks
175g (6oz) unsalted butter, cut into cubes (see tip)
salt and freshly ground black pepper

1 To make the hollandaise sauce, first measure the lemon juice and vinegar into a saucepan, add the egg yolks and mix together. Put the pan on a very low heat and, using a small sauce whisk, gradually whisk in the cubes of butter, continuing to whisk until the butter is incorporated and the sauce is starting to thicken. Season with salt and pepper. Once all the butter has been added, the sauce should be glossy and thick enough to coat the back of a spoon, but be careful not to let it get too hot or it may curdle. Set aside, keeping warm.

2 Bring two saucepans of water to the boil – one large and the other small but deep. Add the broccoli to the large one and boil for 3–5 minutes until al dente, then drain and keep warm.

3 Reduce the heat under the other pan of boiling water to a simmer. Crack an egg on to a small plate and gently slide into the simmering water, then reduce the heat to low, swirling the water around the edges to give the poaching egg a neat shape. Simmer for about 3 minutes or until the white is opaque. Lift out with a slotted spoon and drain, then place on a plate lined with kitchen paper to absorb any excess water and cover to keep warm. Repeat with the other eggs.

4 Divide the cooked broccoli spears between six plates and season with salt and pepper. Place a poached egg on top of each, season again and spoon over the warm hollandaise sauce, finishing with a scattering of black pepper.

TIP
Rather than using the butter straight from the fridge, bring the cubes to room temperature before adding them to the hollandaise – the sauce will thicken more quickly.

Garlic mushrooms and cured ham on toasted brioche

These are perfect for a quick starter or light lunch. Use a variety of mixed wild mushrooms, such as enoki, buna-shimeji, golden enoki, shiitake or oyster. These are widely available now (see tip).

Serves 6

1 tbsp oil
6 slices of dry-cured ham, halved
50g (2oz) butter
6 thick slices of brioche
4 fat garlic cloves, crushed
250g (9oz) chestnut mushrooms, sliced
100g (4oz) shiitake mushrooms, halved if large
75g (3oz) oyster mushrooms, halved if large
150g (5oz) enoki mushrooms or similar (see tip)
2 tbsp full-fat crème fraîche
salt and freshly ground black pepper
chopped parsley, to garnish

1 Add the oil to a large, heavy-based frying pan and fry the ham over a high heat for 1–2 minutes until frazzled and crisp. You may need to do this in two batches so as not to overcrowd the pan. Remove from the pan and set aside.

2 Turn the heat down to medium and melt about a third of the butter in the pan. Add the brioche slices and fry – again, in two batches, if needed – until golden on each side. Remove from the pan and set aside.

3 Melt another third of the butter in the pan, add the garlic, chestnut and shiitake mushrooms and fry over a high heat for 2–3 minutes. Lower the heat, cover with a lid and cook for a further 2 minutes, then remove the lid and fry over a high heat until tender and golden, tossing until dry and any liquid has evaporated.

4 Add the remaining butter, along with the oyster and enoki mushrooms, and fry for a further 1–2 minutes until golden. Season well with salt and pepper and stir in the crème fraîche.

5 Place a slice of toasted brioche on each plate, spoon over some of the garlic mushrooms, followed by a slice of fried ham and a sprinkling of chopped parsley. Serve immediately.

TIPS
Brioche loaves are now sold in most supermarkets.

Enoki mushrooms can usually be purchased in supermarkets in a wild mushroom selection box.

SMOKED TROUT, AVOCADO AND TOMATO TIANS

THESE ARE A LITTLE BIT DIFFERENT and so easy to put together. As they need to be prepared in advance and chilled, they are perfect for entertaining when it makes life easier to have the first course made well ahead and ready to serve. Also pictured overleaf.

SERVES 8

PREPARE AHEAD
These can be made up to 1 day ahead and kept in the fridge.

400g (14oz) cold smoked trout slices (see tip)
2 good handfuls of mixed leaves, to garnish

FOR THE FILLING
3 medium, ripe avocados, peeled, stoned and cut into tiny dice
juice of 1 lemon
2 spring onions, finely chopped
2–3 tomatoes, deseeded and cut into tiny dice
4 tbsp full-fat mayonnaise
4 tbsp full-fat cream cheese
1 tsp Dijon mustard
salt and freshly ground black pepper

1 To make the filling, add the diced avocados to a bowl and mix with the lemon juice, spring onions and half the diced tomatoes. In a separate bowl, mix together the mayonnaise, cream cheese and mustard, season with salt and pepper and stir into the avocado mixture.

2 Wet the inside of eight oval or round ramekins and line with enough cling film so that some overhangs the sides. Line the base and side of each ramekin with a single layer of smoked trout, leaving a little overhanging the sides.

3 Divide half the avocado mixture between the ramekins and press down with the back of a spoon. Scatter with the remaining diced tomatoes to give a red layer, and press down. Top with the remaining avocado mixture, pressing down with the back of a spoon and smoothing the tops.

4 Fold over the overhanging bits of smoked trout and cling film and press down lightly. Chill in the fridge for a minimum of 6 hours or ideally overnight. There is no need to weight down the tops of the tians while they are chilling – they will hold their shape well enough when they are turned out.

5 To serve, unwrap the cling film from the top of each dish and upend the tian on to an individual plate, removing the ramekin and the cling film. Garnish each plate with a few dressed leaves and serve chilled with brown bread or rolls.

TIP
Cold smoked trout comes in vacuum packs. If you can't find smoked trout, you could use smoked salmon.

GOLDEN GOAT'S CHEESE, BEETROOT AND SQUASH SALAD

THIS IS PERFECT FOR A FIRST COURSE or a light lunch as the goat's cheese can be prepared ahead and just pan-fried to serve. Firm goat's cheese with a rind is what you'll need for this recipe. The balsamic glaze used here is a thicker, sweeter variety of balsamic vinegar that is readily available from supermarkets and comes in a squeegee bottle. Also pictured overleaf.

SERVES 6

PREPARE AHEAD
All the components for the salad can be prepared ahead on the day and the goat's cheese coated and kept chilled in the fridge until ready to fry.

1 x 300g roll of firm goat's cheese with a rind, such as chèvre
plain flour, for coating
1 egg
50g (2oz) panko breadcrumbs
30g (1oz) pumpkin seeds
½ tsp coarse sea salt
½ butternut squash, peeled, deseeded and cut into 2cm (¾in) cubes (about 400g/14oz prepared weight)
3 tbsp olive oil
1 x 100g bag of mixed salad leaves
250g (9oz) cooked beetroot, diced
salt and freshly ground black pepper
ready-made balsamic glaze, to serve

1 Put the goat's cheese in the freezer for 15 minutes to firm up. Next remove any thick rind from each end of the roll and cut the cheese into six equal-sized slices, about 2cm (¾in) thick. Add the flour to a plate and season with salt and pepper, beat the egg in a shallow bowl and sprinkle the breadcrumbs on to another plate. Coat each disc with the seasoned flour, dip into the beaten egg, coat in the breadcrumbs and set aside.

2 Place a large, non-stick frying pan over a medium-high heat, add the pumpkin seeds and sea salt and dry-fry for 3–4 minutes until roasted and starting to pop (see tip). Shake the pan regularly to stop them burning. Remove from the heat and set aside.

3 Cook the squash cubes in boiling, salted water for about 5 minutes, until just tender, then drain.

4 Add 1 tablespoon of the oil to the pan and fry the diced squash for about 3–4 minutes, stirring frequently, until golden on all sides and just tender. Season with salt and pepper and set aside.

5 Divide the salad leaves between six individual plates, scatter the pieces of beetroot and squash around the edges and drizzle over the balsamic glaze.

6 Add the remaining oil to the pan and fry the pieces of goat's cheese over a high heat for 1–2 minutes on each side – frying in batches, if necessary – until golden and crisp. Arrange the goat's cheese in the centre of each plate on top of the salad, and sprinkle with the roasted, salted pumpkin seeds to finish.

TIP
Do not overcook the pumpkin seeds, or they will taste bitter.

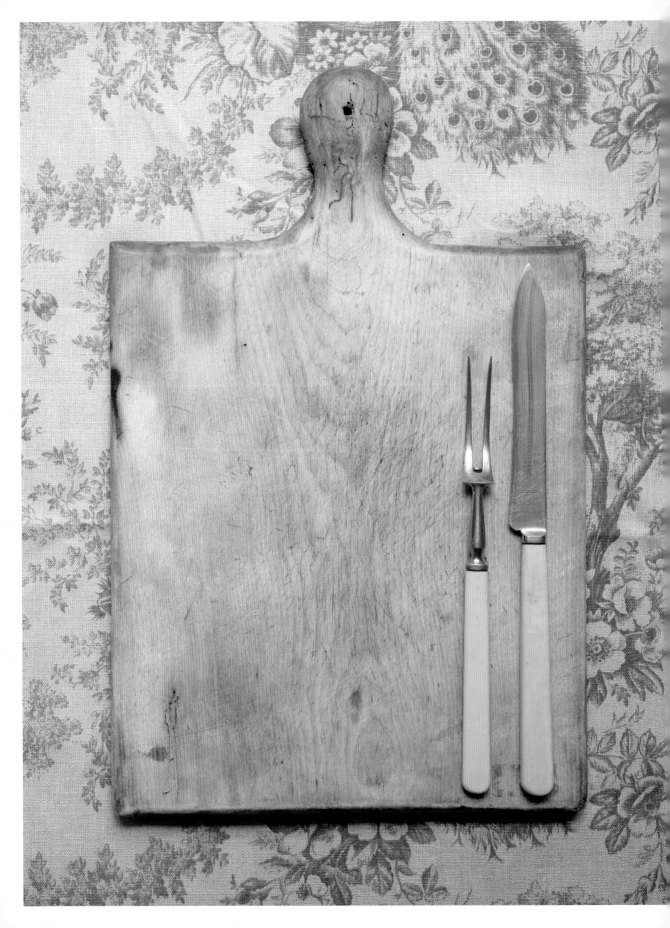

Pork, Beef & Lamb

MEAT DISHES form the traditional cornerstone of a meal and in this chapter I've gathered together some of my all-time favourites, from one-pot dishes that positively benefit from being made ahead so that the flavours develop, to recipes that can be rustled up quickly at the last minute.

Minced beef is one of the most versatile forms of meat, as well as the best value, though I'd always recommend buying the highest quality that you can afford. Here I've used it in my Cottage Pie with Crushed Potato Topping (page 78), to make a nice change from standard mash, and in the Autumn Beef Pie with Filo Crust (page 67), where the crisp pastry contrasts to perfection with the rich mixture of meat and vegetables that make up the filling. Good-quality burgers are in great demand at the moment, especially if homemade (page 77). Adding curry paste to the mix gives a wonderful flavour that's just a bit different and goes down especially well with teenagers, I find, or indeed with anyone who enjoys spicy food.

For dishes to make ahead and especially if you're serving a crowd, I'd recommend the Lamb Fore Shanks with English Vegetables (page 89), full of flavour and yet not overly filling as the cut of meat is slightly smaller than a standard hind leg shank, or the Horseradish and Mustard Beef Casserole (page 92), a real favourite of mine and a wonderfully warming dish that would make a good alternative to turkey at Christmas or to have over the Christmas period.

For warmer days, you could try the Seared Beef and Bean Sprout Salad (page 72), deliciously light and healthy, and if time is of the essence, then pork chops or fillet are ideal. Both the Pork Stroganoff (page 65) and Pork Chops with Mustard Sauce (page 66) can be made at the last minute, yet each would be impressive enough to serve at a dinner party for a small number of people.

ROASTED SAUSAGE AND POTATO SUPPER

THIS WILL BECOME A FIRM FAMILY FAVOURITE as it can be cooked in one dish and is so quick and easy to put together. If you're making this for young children, you can replace the wine with stock, if you prefer. Choose your favourite type of local, British sausage for this recipe – my family loves leek and sage.

SERVES 4–6

2 tbsp olive oil
2 large onions, sliced lengthways
    into wedges
2 red peppers, deseeded and cut
    into large dice
2 garlic cloves, chopped
1 tbsp chopped thyme leaves
500g (1lb 2oz) baby new potatoes,
    unpeeled and halved
12 sausages, pricked with a fork
200ml (7fl oz) white wine
salt and freshly ground black pepper

1 Preheat the oven to 220°C/200°C fan/Gas 7.

2 Place all the ingredients except the wine in a large, resealable freezer bag. Seal the bag shut and shake well to coat everything in the oil. Alternatively, put everything in a large bowl and turn the ingredients until they are fully coated in the oil. Tip into a large roasting tin, spreading the ingredients out into one even layer and ensuring that the sausages aren't covered by any of the vegetables. Season well with salt and pepper.

3 Roast for about 30–35 minutes until golden, then remove from the oven, turn the sausages over and toss the vegetables in the cooking juices. Pour in the wine and return to the oven for a further 20 minutes or until browned and the sausages are cooked and the potatoes tender. Serve hot with a dollop of mustard on the side.

PORK STROGANOFF

A CLASSIC RECIPE that makes an authentic-tasting, meaty dish bound with a creamy sauce and flavoured with plenty of paprika. It's one I often turn to if I am short of time as it can be quickly prepared on the hob. Serve accompanied with boiled basmati rice.

SERVES 4–6

PREPARE AHEAD
The ingredients can be prepared a couple of hours before serving and kept in the fridge.

500g (1lb 2oz) pork fillet
2 tbsp sunflower oil
25g (1oz) butter
1 onion, finely sliced
3 tsp paprika
300g (11oz) button mushrooms, halved
200ml (7fl oz) full-fat crème fraîche or double cream
1 tbsp lemon juice
salt and freshly ground black pepper
1 tbsp chopped parsley, to garnish

1 Remove and discard any membrane from the pork fillet. Cut the meat on the diagonal into 1 x 6cm (½ x 2½in) strips.

2 Heat a large, non-stick frying pan until very hot and add the oil. Fry the meat quickly over the high heat for 3–4 minutes until golden and cooked through, taking care not to overcook. Lift out with a slotted spoon on to a plate.

3 Add the butter to the pan, followed by the sliced onion. Fry for a minute, then lower the heat, cover with a lid and cook for about 10 minutes until the onion is really tender.

4 Sprinkle in the paprika and stir in the mushrooms, then turn up the heat and toss for a minute. Add the pork to the pan with the crème fraîche, allowing to just bubble to heat through, then add the lemon juice and season with salt and pepper. Serve at once, garnished with the chopped parsley, with basmati rice alongside.

Pork chops with mustard sauce

THIS IS AN EASY BUT IMPRESSIVE-LOOKING DISH, one that needs to be cooked and served immediately. The apple flavour in the sauce really comes through well, complementing the pork. Serve with mash and a green vegetable.

SERVES 4

2 tbsp olive oil
4 x 350g (12oz) T-bone pork chops
a large knob of butter
250g (9oz) chestnut mushrooms, sliced
200ml (7fl oz) apple juice
150ml (5fl oz) double cream
2 tbsp grainy mustard
1 tbsp cornflour
salt and freshly ground black pepper

1 Heat the oil in a large frying pan. Add the pork chops and fry over a high heat for 5–7 minutes on each side until golden brown and just cooked through. Using tongs or a pair of forks, turn each chop on to its edge to brown and crisp the rind and fat. Leave to rest in a warm place while you make the sauce.

2 Add the butter to the pan, tip in the mushrooms and fry over a high heat for 3–4 minutes, then season with salt and pepper. Pour in the apple juice, bring to the boil and allow to bubble for 2 minutes to reduce. Add the cream and mustard and return to the boil, stirring constantly. Mix the cornflour with 1 tablespoon of water and then add to the sauce. Stir until thickened, adding the pork juices, and check the seasoning.

3 Put the chops on serving plates, spoon over the hot sauce and serve with creamy mash and greens.

Autumn beef pie with filo crust

PERFECT FOR THE FAMILY or for serving a large gathering. To vary the flavour, especially if anyone in your family isn't keen on onion, you could use leeks or fennel instead. It is best made on the same day it will be eaten, though you can prepare a day ahead. Pictured overleaf.

SERVES 6–8

PREPARE AHEAD
The beef can be prepared, up to the end of step 6, and kept in the fridge for up to 24 hours, until you're ready to bake the pie.

FREEZE
The whole dish, uncooked, freezes well.

75g (3oz) butter, melted, for greasing and brushing
3 tbsp oil
2 onions, chopped
1kg (2lb 3oz) lean minced beef
2 garlic cloves, crushed
2 tbsp plain flour
2 x 400g tins of chopped tomatoes
4 tbsp tomato purée
1 tsp sugar
500g (1lb 2oz) courgettes, cut into 1cm (½in) slices
300g (11oz) full-fat cream cheese
1 tbsp snipped chives
1 tbsp chopped parsley
100g (4oz) Cheddar cheese, grated
1 x 190g jar of roasted red peppers in oil, drained and cut into large pieces
8 sheets of filo pastry
salt and freshly ground black pepper

1 You will need a shallow 2-litre (3½-pint) ovenproof dish. Preheat the oven to 180°C/160°C fan/Gas 4 and grease the dish with a little of the melted butter.

2 Heat 1 tablespoon of the oil in a non-stick, ovenproof frying pan and fry the onions over a high heat for a couple of minutes. Add the mince to the pan and brown all over for 4–5 minutes, breaking up the larger lumps with a wooden spoon. Stir in the garlic and sprinkle over the flour, then mix in the chopped tomatoes, tomato purée and sugar and season with salt and pepper.

3 Bring to the boil, cover with a lid and transfer to the oven to cook for about 45 minutes until the mince is tender.

4 Meanwhile, heat the remaining oil in a separate frying pan, add the courgettes and fry over a high heat for 4–5 minutes until golden – you may need to do this in batches. Season with salt and pepper and set aside.

5 Place the cream cheese in a bowl, add the herbs and season with salt and pepper, stirring to combine.

6 Remove the cooked mince from the oven and increase the temperature to 200°C/180°C fan/Gas 6. Spread the mince over the base of the prepared ovenproof dish and leave to cool. Dollop the cream cheese mixture over the top of the meat and scatter over the grated Cheddar, arrange the courgettes over the cheese and lay the peppers on top.

CONTINUED OVERLEAF

7 Brush each sheet of filo with melted butter. Lay two sheets flat over the top of the dish, side by side, to give one layer of pastry (see tip). Scrunch each of the remaining six sheets into a rosette shape and arrange in two rows on top of the first layer. Brush the filo with more melted butter.

8 Slide the completed dish on to a baking sheet and place in the oven to bake for 25–30 minutes until golden and bubbling. If it starts getting too brown during cooking, cover with a sheet of foil. Serve hot with a dressed salad.

TIP
The size of filo pastry sheets varies, depending on the make. Mine were 25cm square. If your sheets are large, cut them in half to make the scrunchy rosette topping.

MEATBALLS IN TOMATO AND BASIL SAUCE

I FIND THESE GREAT FUN TO MAKE with the grandchildren – they love getting their hands stuck in! The meatballs can be made in advance and sit happily in their sauce until ready to be reheated.

MAKES 24 MEATBALLS/SERVES 6

PREPARE AHEAD
These can be made up to 1 day ahead and kept in the fridge, covered.

FREEZE
The meatballs can be frozen raw. Freeze the sauce separately.

FOR THE MEATBALLS
1 large onion, finely chopped
2–3 garlic cloves, crushed
50g (2oz) Parmesan cheese, grated
1 tbsp thyme leaves, chopped
½ tsp paprika
1 small egg, beaten
500g (1lb 2oz) lean minced beef
2 tbsp olive oil, for frying
salt and freshly ground black pepper

FOR THE SAUCE
1 large onion, chopped
4 garlic cloves, crushed
600ml (1 pint) passata
3 tbsp tomato purée
2 tsp caster sugar
a dash of hot pepper sauce such as
    Tabasco, or ¼ tsp cayenne pepper
2 tbsp chopped basil

1 To make the meatballs, put all the ingredients except the oil in a large bowl, season well with salt and pepper and mix with your hands until combined. It is easier to have damp hands for doing the mixing. Shape into 24 even-sized balls and chill in the fridge for 30 minutes.

2 Heat the oil in wide, heavy-based frying pan, add the meatballs and fry over a high heat, turning with a fork and spoon, for 8–10 minutes or until just golden brown. You will need to do this in batches in order not to overcrowd the pan. The meatballs don't need to be cooked through at this stage, just enough to seal and brown all over. Remove with a slotted spoon and sit on kitchen paper to absorb any excess oil.

3 To make the sauce, return the same pan to the heat (no need to add more oil), add the onion and garlic and fry over a high heat for 10 minutes, then lower the heat, cover with a lid and cook for a further 10 minutes.

4 Stir in the passata, tomato purée, sugar and hot pepper sauce or cayenne pepper, add 300ml (10fl oz) of water (see tip) and season with salt and pepper. Let the sauce bubble, uncovered, for 10 minutes until slightly reduced, then add the meatballs and half the chopped basil. Cover again with the lid and simmer for 10–12 minutes, stirring occasionally, until the meatballs are cooked through. Serve piping hot with spaghetti and with the rest of the basil sprinkled over.

TIP
Pour the 300ml (10fl oz) of water into the empty passata container and swill around gently to remove every remnant of tomato juice before adding to the dish.

Seared beef and bean sprout salad

Fresh, light and healthy, this would be ideal for a summer lunch. To save time on the day, the salad and dressing can be prepared a few hours ahead and the beef cooked just before you're ready to serve.

SERVES 6

PREPARE AHEAD
The dressing can be made 2–3 days in advance and stored in a sealed container. Because bean sprouts have a short shelf life and carry a risk of food poisoning, they should be eaten within 24 hours. The salad can be prepared a few hours in advance. Cook the beef just before serving.

2 x 250g (9oz) rump or sirloin
  steaks, trimmed of fat
2 tbsp sesame seeds, toasted

FOR THE DRESSING
3 tbsp dark soy sauce
3 tbsp light muscovado sugar
juice of 2 limes (see tip)
1 tsp fish sauce
4 tbsp olive oil

FOR THE SALAD
½ cucumber, unpeeled
2 Little Gem lettuces, each cut
  into 6 wedges lengthways through
  the root
3 large carrots, sliced into matchsticks
200g (7oz) fresh bean sprouts, rinsed
2 heaped tbsp chopped mint

1   For the dressing, pour the soy sauce into a jug and mix with the sugar, lime juice and fish sauce. Pour half into a large bowl or platter to use as a marinade. Add the olive oil to the jug, mix well and set aside to use as a dressing. Add the steaks to the marinade in the bowl and leave to marinate for a maximum of 30 minutes. Drain, keeping the marinade.

2   While the steaks are marinating, prepare the salad. Using a wide-bladed potato peeler, peel the cucumber into ribbon-like strips. Tip into a large serving bowl, add the other salad ingredients and toss with your hands to combine.

3   Heat a non-stick frying pan over a high heat, add the marinated steaks and sear for just 1 minute on each side so that the beef is still slightly pink. (Fry for 2–3 minutes per side for more well-cooked steak, if you prefer.) Set aside for 5 minutes to rest. Add the saved marinade to the pan, bring to the boil, then add to the jug of dressing. Slice each steak into thin strips.

4   Arrange the beef over the salad, scatter with the toasted sesame seeds and pour over the dressing from the jug to serve.

TIP
To get the most juice from a lime, either roll it on the work surface to soften it or put in the microwave on high for 20–30 seconds. Allow to cool slightly before cutting. This will release much more juice.

CHILLI BURGERS

THESE ARE SPICY BURGERS with a wonderful savoury flavour from the Thai curry paste. Teenagers seem to love chilli, so if yours like it hot add extra! Alternatively, you could omit the chilli and curry paste and add mustard instead.

SERVES 6

PREPARE AHEAD
The burgers can be prepared in advance and stored, uncooked, in the fridge for up to 2 days before using.

FREEZE
The uncooked burgers can be frozen, wrapped, for up to 2 months.

450g (1lb) best minced steak
1 small onion, finely chopped
2 small red chillies, deseeded and finely chopped
3 tsp Thai red curry paste
1 tbsp chopped parsley
olive or sunflower oil, for brushing
salt and freshly ground black pepper

TO SERVE
ciabatta buns
soured cream or mayonnaise
rocket leaves
sliced tomato
sliced jalapeño peppers (optional)

1 In a large bowl, mix the steak with chopped onion, chillies, curry paste and parsley and season with plenty of salt and pepper. Mix with your hands to ensure all the spices are evenly distributed.

2 Wet your hands and shape into six even-sized, flat patties about 2.5cm (1in) thick.

3 Preheat a ridged griddle pan or non-stick frying pan over a high heat. Brush each side of the burgers with oil and cook for 3–4 minutes on each side. Lift out of the pan as soon as they are cooked right through (which will depend on the thickness of each burger).

4 Assemble each burger in a ciabatta bun with a dollop of soured cream, a few rocket leaves, a few slices of tomato and some slices of jalapeño pepper, if you like.

COTTAGE PIE WITH CRUSHED POTATO TOPPING

THIS CLASSIC RECIPE uses crushed potatoes as a topping, instead of the standard mash, to make a nice change. Also pictured overleaf.

SERVES 6–8

PREPARE AHEAD
The assembled dish can be kept, covered, in the fridge for up to 24 hours before cooking in the oven. Once cooked, it can be stored in the fridge for 1–2 days.

FREEZE
The mince is best frozen without the topping as the potato will lose its texture. Defrost the meat and top with fresh potato as required.

1 tbsp sunflower oil
1kg (2lb 3oz) lean minced beef
2 onions, chopped
4 celery sticks, finely diced
50g (2oz) plain flour
300ml (10fl oz) red wine
300ml (10fl oz) beef stock
1 tbsp Worcestershire sauce
1 tbsp redcurrant jelly
1 tbsp chopped thyme leaves
a dash of gravy browning
salt and freshly ground black pepper

FOR THE TOPPING
800g (1¾lb) new potatoes,
  unpeeled and scrubbed
about 3 tbsp olive oil

1 You will need a shallow 2-litre (3½-pint) ovenproof dish. Preheat the oven to 160°C/140°C fan/Gas 3.

2 Heat the oil in a deep, ovenproof frying pan or sauté pan, add the mince and brown over a high heat for about 5 minutes, stirring and breaking up the meat with a wooden spoon until no pink remains. Add the onions and celery to the mince, and fry over a high heat for a further 3–4 minutes.

3 Sprinkle in the flour and fry, stirring for a minute, then stir in the remaining ingredients and season with salt and pepper. Bring to the boil, then cover with a lid and transfer to the oven to cook for about 1½ hours or until tender.

4 While the meat is cooking, place the potatoes in a saucepan of salted water, bring to the boil and boil for 15–20 minutes until just tender. Drain, return to the pan and, using a fork, break the potatoes into large rough chunks. Drizzle in the olive oil and some salt and pepper, and toss to coat well. Set aside.

5 When the meat is cooked, remove from the oven and increase the temperature to 200°C/180°C fan/Gas 6. Transfer the cooked mince to the ovenproof dish and spoon over the crushed potatoes. Place the dish in the oven and bake for 30–40 minutes or until bubbling and golden-tinged on top.

Rib-eye steak with green peppercorn sauce

THIS SAUCE WOULD GO WELL with any cut of steak, though my favourites are rib-eye, as here, and fillet, as they are so tender and need only a short amount of cooking.

SERVES 6

PREPARE AHEAD
The sauce can be made up to a day ahead, kept in the fridge and reheated to serve. If a little thick, add a touch more cream or stock to thin to the correct consistency while heating.

6 x 200g (7oz) rib-eye steaks
oil, for frying

FOR THE SAUCE
a knob of butter
2 shallots, finely diced
75ml (3fl oz) brandy
300ml (10fl oz) double cream
1 rounded tsp Dijon mustard
1½ tsp green peppercorns, in brine, drained and chopped
a pinch of sugar
salt and freshly ground black pepper
watercress, to garnish

1   To make the sauce, melt the butter in a frying pan, add the shallots and fry over a medium-high heat for about 5 minutes or until soft. Pour in the brandy and boil for 30 seconds to reduce, then add the cream, mustard, peppercorns and sugar. Season with salt and pepper and allow to bubble, stirring all the while, until slightly thickened. Set aside, keeping warm.

2   Preheat a ridged, cast-iron chargrill pan or heavy-based frying pan over a high heat for 5–10 minutes, until piping hot. Brush the steaks with oil on both sides and season with pepper.

3   Place the steaks in the pan and grill or fry for 2–3 minutes on each side for rare to medium-rare meat (or 4 minutes on the first side and 2–3 minutes on the second, for medium to well done). Lift the steaks out of the pan, season with salt and more pepper if required, and let them rest. Serve hot with the green peppercorn sauce and a watercress garnish.

TIPS
I love the softer green peppercorns, but you could use half the amount of ground black peppercorns, if you prefer.

The steaks should be left on the side to come to room temperature before cooking. Do not cook them from chilled or they will be disappointingly tough.

Harissa spiced lamb with cannellini beans

This rustic lamb casserole is full of flavour, especially if made ahead, and the lamb is meltingly tender. Harissa is a chilli paste with quite a kick; rose harissa, which I prefer to use, is sweeter and less fiery due to the addition of rose petals. I don't like my food too spicy, so this dish is mild, but if you prefer it hot just add more harissa and good luck! The inclusion of the beans means you only need to serve with a green vegetable. If you omit the beans, serve with rice or couscous. A little soured cream helps to counterbalance the spiciness of the dish if you're adding extra harissa.

SERVES 6

PREPARE AHEAD
Make up to 2 days ahead as the flavours will continue to develop.

FREEZE
This dish freezes well.

4 tbsp olive oil
2 tbsp ground cumin
2 tbsp ground coriander
1kg (2lb 3oz) lamb neck fillet, trimmed and cut into small pieces
2.5cm (1in) knob of fresh root ginger, finely grated (see tip)
2 onions, thinly sliced
250ml (9fl oz) white wine
1 x 400g tin of chopped tomatoes
2 tbsp tomato purée
2 tbsp runny honey
1½ tbsp harissa paste (preferably rose)
finely grated rind and juice of ½ lemon
1 x 400g tin of cannellini beans, drained and rinsed
salt and freshly ground black pepper

1 Preheat the oven to 160°C/140°C fan/Gas 3.

2 Heat 2 tablespoons of the oil in a deep, ovenproof frying pan or flameproof casserole dish. Sprinkle the cumin and coriander over the lamb pieces and fry in two batches in the hot oil for about 5 minutes or until browned. Remove with a slotted spoon and set aside.

3 Pour the remaining oil into the pan, add the ginger and onions and fry over a high heat for 10 minutes until soft. Pour in the wine and boil for 2–3 minutes, stirring and scraping the bottom of the pan to incorporate all the caramelised meaty bits.

4 Add all the remaining ingredients, except the beans, and stir well, then return the lamb to the pan, season with salt and pepper and bring to the boil.

5 Cover with a lid and transfer to the oven to cook for 1¼ hours. Stir in the beans and return to the oven to cook for 15 minutes or until the lamb is tender.

TIPS
There's no need to peel the ginger root if you just trim the ends and then grate it. The skin usually gets left behind, attached to the root, and the pulpy ginger appears on the other side of the grater.

If you need to spin the lamb out for extra-hungry people, add another can of beans to make the casserole go a little further.

LAMB FORE SHANKS WITH ENGLISH VEGETABLES

FOR THIS RECIPE I HAVE USED LAMB FORE SHANKS, taken from the front leg. Although this cut of meat would not be described as shoulder of lamb, it is taken from the overall shoulder area. I find a whole leg shank tends to be too much for one person, whereas a fore shank, being smaller, provides the perfect amount. Ask your butcher for these if you can't find them in the supermarket.

SERVES 6

PREPARE AHEAD
Cook the lamb casserole 1–2 days in advance and prepare the vegetables shortly before serving.

3 tbsp oil
6 x 200g (7oz) lamb fore shanks
2 onions, sliced
2 garlic cloves, crushed
1 rounded tbsp plain flour
300ml (10fl oz) red wine
450ml (15fl oz) chicken stock
1 tbsp redcurrant jelly
1 tbsp chopped rosemary leaves
250g (9oz) baby carrots, cut in half
    lengthways if large
250g (9oz) parsnips, cut into batons
250g (9oz) baby turnips, cut in half
    lengthways if large
a knob of butter
salt and freshly ground black pepper
2 tbsp chopped parsley, to garnish

1   Preheat the oven to 160°C/140°C fan/Gas 3.

2   Heat 2 tablespoons of the oil in a deep, ovenproof frying pan or flameproof casserole dish and brown the lamb shanks all over on a high heat for 5–6 minutes or until golden. Remove with a slotted spoon and set aside.

3   Add the remaining oil and the onion and garlic and fry over a medium heat for 3–4 minutes until soft. Measure the flour into a bowl, pour in the wine and whisk into a smooth paste. Add the stock to the onions, then add the wine and flour mix and, stirring continuously, bring to the boil. Add the redcurrant jelly and rosemary and stir until thickened.

4   Place the browned lamb back in the pan, season with salt and pepper, then cover with a lid and transfer to the oven to cook for about 2 hours or until the lamb is tender and just falling off the bone.

5   When ready to serve, bring a saucepan of salted water to the boil, add the carrots, parsnips and turnips and boil for 8–10 minutes or until tender. Drain.

6   Add a third of the vegetables to the lamb casserole and stir. Melt a knob of butter in a frying pan and fry the remaining vegetables over a high heat for 4–5 minutes or until golden, season with salt and pepper and remove from the hob.

7   Serve one fore shank per person with some of the sauce and vegetables from the casserole and extra fried vegetables on the side. Garnish with the chopped parsley to finish.

TIP
'Batons' is just a posh name for vegetables cut into long strips.

CANON OF LAMB WITH MINT GRAVY

CANON OF LAMB is the tender fillet of loin – so called because it resembles a cannon – and is one of the best cuts for roasting. In this classy, classic recipe it is served with rich mint gravy – perfect for a special occasion. If you are unable to get hold of mint jelly, mix together 1 rounded teaspoon of redcurrant jelly with 1 teaspoon of mint sauce. Serve the lamb with a delicate green vegetable, such as tenderstem broccoli or mangetout.

SERVES 6

PREPARE AHEAD
The lamb can be browned up to 6 hours in advance and cooked to serve. The gravy can be made up to a day ahead.

3 long sprigs of rosemary
1 tbsp oil
3 lamb loin fillets
salt and freshly ground black pepper

FOR THE GRAVY
25g (1oz) butter
1 small onion, finely diced
1 garlic clove, crushed
25g (1oz) plain flour
450ml (15fl oz) hot beef or chicken stock
150ml (5fl oz) port
1 rounded tsp mint jelly
a few drops of gravy browning
1 tbsp chopped mint

1 Preheat the oven to 220°C/200°C fan/Gas 7 and lay the sprigs of rosemary in a roasting tin.

2 Heat the oil in a large frying pan. Season the lamb with salt and pepper and fry the fillets quickly in the hot pan so they are browned on all sides. Arrange on the rosemary sprigs in the roasting tin and then roast in the oven for about 8 minutes (so the lamb is still pink in the middle). Remove from the oven and set aside, still in the tin, to rest.

3 To make the gravy, first melt the butter in a saucepan, add the onion and garlic and fry over a medium heat for 3–4 minutes. Sprinkle in the flour and stir over the heat, then blend in the hot stock, followed by the port. Bring to the boil, stirring until smooth and slightly thickened.

4 Add the mint jelly, gravy browning and chopped mint and season with a little salt and pepper. Stir together, adding any cooking juices from the roasting tin for the lamb, and boil for 1 minute. Strain the gravy through a sieve into a warmed jug.

5 To serve, slice the lamb on the diagonal and spoon over a little gravy.

Horseradish and mustard beef casserole

This is a big, hearty casserole that's made on the hob, so you'll need a large pan with a heavy base suitable for cooking over direct heat for 3 hours. Serve the finished dish piping hot with mash and vegetables of your choice.

Serves 6

Prepare ahead
This can be made up to 2 days ahead and gently reheated.

Freeze
The cooked dish freezes well without the cream.

3 tbsp sunflower oil
1.5kg (3lb) braising beef, diced
3 large onions, roughly chopped
6 garlic cloves, crushed
50g (2oz) plain flour
300ml (10fl oz) white wine
300ml (10fl oz) beef stock
3 tbsp Worcestershire sauce
1 tbsp light muscovado sugar
500g (1lb 2oz) chestnut mushrooms, halved
3 tbsp Dijon mustard
3 tbsp creamed horseradish sauce
3–4 tbsp double cream
salt and freshly ground black pepper
1 tbsp chopped parsley, to garnish

1 Heat 2 tablespoons of the oil in a deep frying pan, large sauté pan or flameproof casserole dish and cook the beef over a high heat for about 5 minutes or until golden brown and sealed – you may need to do this in batches. Using a slotted spoon, remove the meat and set aside.

2 Add the remaining oil to the pan, tip in the onions and garlic and stir well, scraping in the caramelised meaty bits from the bottom of the pan. Fry over a medium-high heat for 5 minutes to soften the onions.

3 Measure the flour and 100ml (3½fl oz) of the wine into a bowl and whisk until smooth, then pour in the remaining wine and stir to combine.

4 Return the browned beef to the pan, pour in the beef stock, then the wine and flour blend and bring to the boil, stirring until thickened. Add the Worcestershire sauce and sugar and season with salt and pepper. Bring back to the boil, stirring, cover with a lid and simmer over a low heat for 2 hours, stirring from time to time. Add the mushrooms, bring back to the boil, cover and simmer for a further 30 minutes until the meat is tender.

5 Mix the mustard, horseradish and double cream together in a bowl and stir into the casserole. Garnish with chopped parsley to finish.

TIPS
At first it may seem that there is not enough liquid in this recipe, and even that it will need to be topped up during the cooking time. But there is no need to: when the mushrooms are added, they release a lot of water, which adds to the rich gravy.

If you like a hotter flavour, add hot horseradish sauce or double the amount of creamed horseradish sauce.

Sage and onion stuffing balls

These provide the perfect accompaniment to roast poultry. The stuffing mixture can otherwise be used to stuff the neck end of a 6–7½kg (14–17lb) turkey or the cavity of two large chickens.

Makes 12 balls

Prepare ahead
These can be made a day ahead and gently reheated.

Freeze
The raw balls freeze well.

40g (1½oz) butter
1 large onion, chopped
750g (1¾lb) pork sausage meat
150g (5oz) fresh white breadcrumbs
juice and finely grated rind of
    1 large lemon
3 tbsp chopped parsley
1 tbsp chopped sage
1 tbsp oil
salt and freshly ground black pepper

1 Preheat the oven to 200°C/180°C fan/Gas 6.

2 Melt the butter in a saucepan, add the onion and cook gently for about 10 minutes until soft. Stir in the remaining ingredients except the oil and mix well together. Season with salt and pepper and shape into 12 even-sized balls.

3 Heat the oil in a large frying pan and brown the balls over a high heat, turning them, for 4–5 minutes until golden. Transfer to a baking tray or, if making to accompany a roast chicken or turkey (page 122), place in the roasting tin next to the bird, if there is room. Bake for 20 minutes or until cooked through.

TIP
I find it easier to shape the stuffing balls when I have damp hands.

Poultry &
Game

CHICKEN MUST BE THE MOST VERSATILE of meats, which is why I've devoted virtually a whole chapter to it. However, I have also included a recipe for turkey crown (page 122) – an excellent substitute for a whole turkey at Christmas that would suit a smaller family – and a couple of delicious game dishes.

What I love about chicken is the way in which it can be dressed up for a special occasion, or down for a comforting family meal. Because it's a relatively bland meat, it combines to perfection with other flavours, as in the fresh and flavoursome Chicken with Asparagus and Lemon Crème Fraîche Sauce (page 100), which is a particular favourite of mine and ideal for a dinner party. The Pesto Lemon Chicken (page 109) is a salad dish that could also be served at a more formal gathering, such as a buffet party, as it looks so eye-catching once assembled on the plate.

To really wow your guests, you could try the Spatchcock Poussins with Orange, Sage and Ginger (page 110), the meat

bursting with flavour from long marinating, or the Raised
Chicken and Ham Pie (page 119), a bit more fiddly to prepare
but really worth the effort and just right for a cold buffet or
picnic. By contrast, the Sticky Chicken (page 104) is dead easy
to put together and, like the Mediterranean Chicken Thighs
(page 102), would provide a wonderfully tasty dish for a
family meal.

Pheasant tends to be associated with a whole roasted bird,
with a lot of time-consuming plucking to make it ready for
the oven, but pheasant breasts are available from some good
supermarkets and take very little time to prepare. Here I've
cooked them in a mushroom and paprika sauce (page 114) –
piquant and creamy and totally indulgent. The Venison
Casserole with Cherry and Red Wine Sauce (page 117) is
another favourite, well worth making a couple of days ahead
as the flavours intensify gloriously with keeping.

CHICKEN WITH ASPARAGUS AND LEMON CRÈME FRAÎCHE SAUCE

THIS RECIPE IS VERY EASY to make ahead and can be cooked either in the oven or on the hob. Served with rice or baby new potatoes, this would make a perfect dinner party dish.

SERVES 6

PREPARE AHEAD
Can be prepared ahead of time up to the end of step 4. Cook the asparagus when ready to serve, so it keeps fresh and bright green in colour, and add to the reheated chicken with the crème fraîche and parsley.

50g (2oz) butter
2 tbsp oil
6 small skinless, boneless chicken breasts
6 banana shallots, quartered lengthways
30g (1oz) plain flour
400ml (14fl oz) chicken stock
1½ tbsp chopped lemon thyme leaves
12 asparagus spears, woody ends snapped off
juice of 1 large lemon
200ml (7fl oz) full-fat crème fraîche (see tip)
2 tbsp chopped parsley
salt and freshly ground black pepper

1 Preheat the oven (if not cooking this dish on the hob) to 180°C/160°C fan/Gas 4.

2 Heat half the butter and half the oil in a large, deep, ovenproof frying pan or flameproof casserole dish. Season the chicken breasts with salt and pepper and fry in the hot fat for 2 minutes on each side until golden. It's best to do this in two batches if they don't all fit in one pan. Remove from the pan and set aside.

3 Add the remaining butter and oil to the pan, tip in the shallots and fry over a high heat for 5–10 minutes or until lightly golden.

4 Measure the flour into a bowl, whisk in 8 tablespoons of the stock and mix until smooth. Add to the pan and bring to the boil, then pour in the remaining stock. Add the chopped thyme and return the chicken to the pan. Cover with a lid and either cook in the oven for about 20 minutes or gently simmer over a medium heat on the hob for about 20 minutes or until the chicken is cooked through.

5 Just before serving, trim the tip from each asparagus spear and slice the stem into short, even lengths. Cook the asparagus tips and sliced stems in boiling salted water for 2–3 minutes. Drain, reserving the 12 asparagus tips for garnishing the finished dish.

6 Stir the lemon juice, crème fraîche and chopped parsley into the pan with the chicken. Add the sliced asparagus stems and bring to the boil, then remove the chicken, slice each breast into three and arrange on a plate. Spoon over the sauce and arrange two asparagus tips in a cross over the top.

TIP
Do take care to use full-fat crème fraîche. If you can't get hold of any, you could substitute half the quantity of double cream.

MEDITERRANEAN CHICKEN THIGHS

A WARMING, HEARTY DISH that's great for the family and easily multiplied to serve a mass of people. The aubergine melts in the mouth and the tomato sauce is rich and tasty. Serve with mash or rice and a green vegetable or with crusty bread and a salad.

SERVES 6

PREPARE AHEAD
This dish can be made a day in advance and kept in the fridge. Omit the cheese from the top and scatter over when ready to reheat, so it is freshly melted and golden.

2 tbsp olive oil
12 skinless, boneless chicken
   thighs
150g (5oz) chorizo sausage,
   halved lengthways and sliced
2 onions, sliced
1 aubergine, halved lengthways
   and sliced
1 red pepper, deseeded and cut
   into 2cm (¾in) cubes
2 garlic cloves, crushed
650ml (1 pint 2fl oz) passata
2 tbsp tomato purée
2 tsp light muscovado sugar
75g (3oz) pitted black olives
25g (1oz) each of Parmesan and
   Cheddar cheese, grated
salt and freshly ground black
   pepper

1   Preheat the oven to 180°C/160°C fan/Gas 4.

2   Heat a deep, ovenproof frying pan, and add the oil. When the oil is hot, add the chicken thighs and fry over a high heat for 2 minutes on each side or until golden brown all over – you may need to do this in batches. Remove with tongs or a slotted spoon and set aside.

3   Add the chorizo to the frying pan, fry for about 5 minutes until crisp, then remove with a slotted spoon and set aside with the chicken. Add the onions, aubergine, red pepper and garlic and fry over a high heat for a few minutes or until starting to soften.

4   Add the passata, tomato purée and sugar and season with salt and pepper. Bring to the boil and add the browned chicken thighs and fried chorizo with the olives. Cover with a lid, bring to the boil and transfer to the oven to bake for about 30 minutes or until the chicken is just cooked.

5   Remove the lid, scatter the cheeses over the top and return to the oven (without the lid) for 10 minutes until the cheeses have melted and are bubbling and golden.

STICKY CHICKEN

QUICK AND EASY TO MAKE, this is a dish that teenagers will love. I've used skinless chicken breasts here, but it would also work well with breasts with the skin left on or with chicken thighs. Serve with dressed rocket leaves and the Potato Wedges on page 182. Any leftover chicken is delicious eaten cold the next day, sliced up as part of a salad.

SERVES 6

PREPARE AHEAD
The glaze can be mixed well in advance and kept at room temperature ready to pour over the chicken just before cooking. The peppers can be chopped ahead of time and kept in a freezer bag in the fridge.

oil, for greasing
6 skinless, boneless chicken breasts
(150–175g/5–6oz each)
3 red peppers, deseeded and cut
into large chunks
salt and freshly ground black pepper
2 tbsp chopped parsley, to garnish

FOR THE GLAZE
4 tbsp dark soy sauce
2 tbsp sesame oil
3 tbsp runny honey
4cm (1½in) knob of fresh root
ginger, peeled and finely
chopped (see tip)
1 red chilli, deseeded and
finely chopped

1 Preheat the oven to 200°C/180° fan/Gas 6 and grease a large roasting tin with oil.

2 Arrange the chicken breasts and pepper pieces in the greased tin and season with salt and pepper. Mix all the ingredients for the sticky glaze in a jug or bowl and spoon over the chicken.

3 Roast in the oven for 25 minutes or until the chicken is cooked through and the juices run clear. Baste the meat halfway through cooking.

4 Using a slotted spoon, transfer the chicken and peppers to a serving dish to rest for a few minutes. Put the roasting tin on the hob over a high heat and boil the cooking juices for 3–4 minutes until thickened. (Take care not to let the sugars in the glaze burn as this will make it bitter.) Pour the sticky glaze over the chicken and sprinkle with the chopped parsley to finish.

TIP
To peel the ginger, scrape it with the tip of a teaspoon; it comes away easily as it is so thin and you don't waste any of the ginger flesh.

PESTO LEMON CHICKEN

A TAKE ON THE CLASSIC MEDITERRANEAN TRICOLORE SALAD but with cucumber instead of mozzarella and with added chicken. The chicken is best mixed in the dressing a day ahead to allow the flavours to infuse, while the salad should be made fresh on the day.

SERVES 6

PREPARE AHEAD
The dressing can be prepared
1–2 days in advance.

3 cooked skinless, boneless chicken
   breasts, halved horizontally and
   sliced into thin strips
2 large ripe avocados, peeled and
   sliced
juice of ½ large lemon
½ cucumber
18 baby plum tomatoes, halved
   lengthways

FOR THE DRESSING
4 tbsp fresh green basil pesto
6 tbsp light mayonnaise
juice of ½ large lemon
salt and freshly ground black pepper

TO SERVE
25g (1oz) pine nuts, toasted
micro salad (see tip)
basil leaves

1 To make the dressing, measure the pesto, mayonnaise and lemon juice into a large bowl, season with salt and pepper and mix to combine. Add the chicken and stir again. If possible, leave it to marinate for several hours or overnight.

2 Place the avocado slices in a separate bowl, pour over the lemon juice and toss so the avocado is completely coated.

3 Cut the cucumber in half lengthways, use a teaspoon to remove and discard the seeds and then peel using a potato peeler. Cut into crescent-shaped slices and arrange these in layers with the avocado slices, tomato halves and pesto chicken. Season with salt and pepper. (If assembling ahead, do not add salt until just before serving.)

4 Scatter over the toasted pine nuts, micro salad and basil leaves to finish.

TIPS
Micro salad is as it sounds – mini leaves that are pretty and full of flavour. If you can't get hold of micro salad, then a bag of mixed salad leaves or even watercress would make a good alternative.

Freeze any leftover fresh pesto and use within 1 month.

Spatchcock poussins with orange, sage and ginger

I LOVE THE FLAVOURS IN THIS RECIPE, and have adapted it over the years. As this is a book of my absolute favourites, I had to put it in! A whole poussin is often too much for one person, so I tend to cut them in half once cooked and offer half to begin with. You can use chicken breasts or quarters, if you prefer. As the chicken is left to marinate for 24 hours, this dish is best made a day or so in advance. Also pictured overleaf.

SERVES 6

PREPARE AHEAD
Store in the marinade for up to 2 days in the fridge.

FREEZE
The raw poussins in the marinade can be frozen.

3 x 450g (1lb) poussins
1 tbsp runny honey
1 rounded tbsp cornflour
salt and freshly ground black pepper

FOR THE MARINADE
600ml (1 pint) orange juice
3 fat garlic cloves, crushed
2 tbsp olive oil
4 tbsp soy sauce
1 tbsp chopped sage, plus extra
   leaves to garnish
2 tsp thyme leaves
1 tbsp coarsely grated fresh root
   ginger (see tip on page 84)

1 First cut the backbone out of each poussin. Place the birds, breast side down, on a chopping board and, using a sharp pair of kitchen scissors or shears, cut along either side of the bone to remove completely. Turn over and flatten the poussins by pressing down with your hand over the breast bone.

2 Combine all the marinade ingredients and place in a large, resealable freezer bag with the poussins. Seal the bag and leave the chicken to marinate in the fridge for about 24 hours.

3 When you're ready to cook, preheat the oven to 200°C/180°C fan/ Gas 6.

4 Take the poussins out of the bag, saving the marinade to make the sauce. Arrange the poussins, breast side up, in a large roasting tin and drizzle over the honey.

5 Place in the oven to roast for about 20 minutes. Measure the cornflour into a jug, add the marinade and mix until smooth. Pour the marinade over the poussins and return to the oven to roast for a further 15 minutes.

6 Remove the tin from the oven and cut each poussin in half along the breast bone. Strain the juices left in the tin to make a sauce, seasoning with salt and pepper to taste. Serve half a poussin per person, with some of the sauce spooned over and garnished with sage leaves.

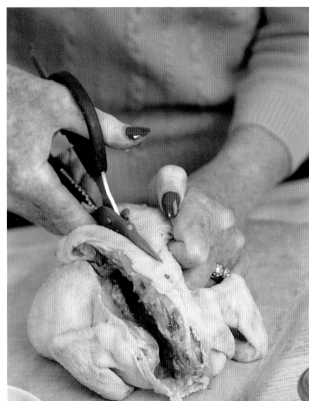

Paprika pheasant breasts with mushroom sauce

Pheasant legs need slow braising in a casserole, but pheasant breasts, available in supermarkets, take much less time to cook. The meat is tender and the sauce creamy, rich and piquant from the paprika. Serve with mash or rice and a seasonal green vegetable.

Serves 6

Prepare ahead
The cooked pheasant and sauce will keep for up to 2 days in the fridge. Reheat to serve.

6 skinless pheasant breasts
50g (2oz) butter
1 large onion, thickly sliced
1 tbsp light muscovado sugar
2 tbsp paprika
300ml (10fl oz) double cream
250g (9oz) chestnut mushrooms, sliced
2 tbsp chopped parsley
salt and freshly ground black pepper

1   Season the pheasant breasts with salt and pepper. Heat a third of the butter in a deep frying pan, add the breasts and cook over a high heat for 3 minutes on one side and 2 minutes on the other, until golden brown all over. You may need to do this in two batches. Remove with a slotted spoon and set aside.

2   Heat half the remaining butter, add the onion and fry over a high heat for 1 minute. Lower the heat, cover the pan with a lid and cook for 5 minutes, stirring occasionally, until nearly soft.

3   Add the sugar and paprika and fry for a minute. Pour in the cream, return the pheasant breasts and any cooking juices to the pan and season with salt and pepper. Cover with the lid and simmer over a medium heat for about 10 minutes or until the pheasant is tender.

4   While the pheasant is cooking, heat the remaining butter in a medium frying pan and fry the mushrooms over a high heat for 2–3 minutes until golden and all the liquid has evaporated. Add the mushrooms and half the parsley to the pan with the pheasant breasts. Serve one breast per person, with some of the sauce poured over and sprinkled with the remaining parsley.

VENISON CASSEROLE WITH CHERRY AND RED WINE SAUCE

THIS IS AN INTENSELY FLAVOURED STEW, rich and full-bodied, that really benefits from being made ahead as the taste improves with keeping. It would go well with mashed potatoes and vegetables of your choice. If you don't have any cherry jam, redcurrant jelly makes a good substitute.

SERVES 6

PREPARE AHEAD
The casserole can be made up to 3 days ahead and reheated to serve.

FREEZE
The cooked dish freezes well.

2lb (1kg) stewing venison, cut into
  2cm (¾in) cubes
1 tsp mixed spice powder
450ml (15fl oz) red wine
2 tbsp olive oil
2 leeks, thickly sliced
25g (1oz) plain flour
300ml (10fl oz) game or beef stock
1 bay leaf
2 tbsp cherry jam
salt and freshly ground black pepper

1 Add the venison cubes to a large bowl, sprinkle in the mixed spice and pour over the wine, then leave to marinate for a minimum of 2 hours.

2 Lift the venison out of the marinade and pat dry. Strain and reserve the marinade left in the bowl.

3 Heat the oil in a large flameproof casserole dish or deep, non-stick frying pan, add the marinated venison and fry over a high heat until well browned – you may need to do this in batches. Using a slotted spoon, remove the venison and set aside.

4 Add the leeks to the dish or pan and fry over a high heat for 1 minute. Sprinkle in the flour and continue to fry, stirring constantly, for a further minute. Gradually pour in the reserved marinade and the stock and bring to the boil, stirring all the time to deglaze the pan. Allow to boil for 2–3 minutes until thickened, then add the bay leaf and cherry jam.

5 Return the venison to the pan, season with salt and pepper and bring to the boil. Lower the heat, cover with a lid and simmer over a low heat for about 2 hours, stirring occasionally, until tender. Remove the bay leaf to serve.

Raised chicken and ham pie

PERFECT SERVED FOR A PICNIC or on Boxing Day, this pie is best made a day or two ahead to ensure it does not crumble when cut. If you like, you could use Christmas leftovers in this pie – replacing the chicken breasts and gammon with the same quantity of cooked turkey and ham.

SERVES 8–10

PREPARE AHEAD
This can be kept, wrapped, in the fridge for 1–2 days.

FOR THE PASTRY
250g (9oz) plain flour, plus extra for dusting
100g (4oz) lard, plus extra for greasing
1 egg, beaten, for brushing

FOR THE FILLING
6 large eggs
450g (1lb) pork sausage meat
1 tbsp chopped thyme leaves
finely grated zest of 1 lemon
4 pickled walnuts, drained, quartered (or smaller if large) and dried
500g (1lb 2oz) skinless, boneless chicken breasts, sliced into thick strips
200g (7oz) piece of gammon steak, sliced into thick strips
salt and freshly ground black pepper

1 You will need a 900g (2lb) loaf tin (see tip overleaf). Preheat the oven to 200°C/180° fan/Gas 6 and grease and line the base and sides of the tin with baking paper, allowing the sides of the paper to come above the edge of the tin.

2 First make the filling. Put the eggs into a saucepan, cover with cold water and bring to the boil. Boil for 8 minutes, then drain, cool in cold water and peel (see tip overleaf). Trim the white ends from the eggs so you can just see the yolk at each end. This means everyone gets a piece with a whole slice of egg – the trimmed ends can be reserved for using in a salad or sandwiches.

3 Mix the sausage meat, thyme and lemon zest together in a large bowl and season with salt and pepper. Cover and set aside.

4 To make the pastry, first measure the flour into a bowl. Pour 100ml (3½fl oz) of water into a saucepan, add the lard and a little salt and bring to the boil. Pour the hot mixture into the bowl with the flour and mix with a spoon until combined, then knead into a dough.

5 Set aside a third of the dough for the lid, wrapping it in cling film. Dust the work surface with flour and roll the remaining two-thirds of the dough into a thin rectangle that's large enough to line the whole of the inside of the tin and come over the edges slightly. Lay the dough in the tin, pushing the pastry into the base and corners of the tin to remove any creases and leaving a little overhanging the edge.

6 With slightly wet hands, press a third (150g/5oz) of the sausage meat mixture into the base of the pastry-lined tin. Put half of the dried pickled walnuts (8–12 pieces) on top, then season the chicken strips with salt and pepper and arrange half (250g/9oz) on top of the walnuts. Spread a thin layer (75g/3oz) of sausage meat on top. Arrange the eggs, end to end, along the centre and push down so

CONTINUED OVERLEAF

they squidge into the sausage meat. Push more sausage meat (75g/3oz) around the side of the eggs and on top of the eggs.

7 Place all the gammon on top – arranging the strips across the width of the tin – and more sausage meat (75g/3oz), making sure there are no gaps. Put the remaining walnuts (8–12 pieces) on top, followed by the remaining chicken and sausage meat. Press down firmly – this is important to ensure the pie does not crumble when it is cut.

8 Roll out the reserved pastry to the size of the top of the pie, brush some of the beaten egg over the pastry overhanging the tin and lay the piece of pastry on top to make a lid. Trim the edges and seal tightly, then crimp the edges and make a tiny hole in the middle to let out the steam. Roll out any pastry trimmings and use these to decorate the top of the pie, attaching them with beaten egg. Brush the top of the pie with more of the beaten egg to finish.

9 Place the tin on a baking tray (to catch any escaping juices and fat) and slide into the oven. Bake for 30 minutes until lightly golden, then reduce the oven temperature to 180°C/160°C fan/Gas 4 and cook for 1 hour until deep golden brown on top and cooked through. Allow to cool completely in the tin, then lift out of the tin using the baking paper and remove. Leave to chill in the fridge overnight and cut into thick slices to serve.

TIPS

To ensure that the pastry browns properly, it's best not to use a loaf tin with insulated base and sides (this type is sold in some cookware shops and will specify 'insulated' on the label).

Ensure the eggs are cooled completely in cold water to prevent a black ring forming around the yolk. Bash the ends of the shell and start peeling at the wider end, where the air gap is, to make the shell easier to remove.

Turkey crown with orange

A TURKEY CROWN is essentially just the breast section of the turkey, with the wings and legs removed. It's an ideal joint if you do not wish to roast a whole bird, easier to carve and with very little wastage too. I like to serve this with my Sprouts with Chestnuts and Pancetta (page 187).

SERVES 8–10

PREPARE AHEAD
The turkey crown can be roasted a day ahead. The gravy can be made a day in advance and reheated until hot.

2.2kg (4lb 14oz) raw turkey crown
2 tsp chopped thyme leaves
50g (2oz) butter, softened
2 small oranges
salt and freshly ground black pepper

FOR THE GRAVY
3 tbsp plain flour
100ml (3½fl oz) port
450ml (15fl oz) hot turkey or chicken stock
a few drops of Worcestershire sauce
2 tbsp soy sauce

1 Preheat the oven to 200°C/180°C fan/Gas 6.

2 First loosen the skin on the turkey crown (see tip). Mix the thyme leaves with the softened butter and spread between the flesh and skin. Thinly slice one orange and arrange the slices under the skin in two neat rows. Cut the second orange in half and place one half under the skin at the neck end of the bird. Place any orange trimmings in the neck cavity.

3 Sit the crown in a small roasting tin and season with salt and pepper. Roast in the oven for about 1½ hours or until the juices run clear when pierced with a skewer. Check the turkey after 30 minutes and cover with foil if getting too brown. Just 15 minutes before the end of cooking, squeeze over the juice from the remaining half-orange and put back in the oven, uncovered, to crisp up.

4 Transfer to a platter and leave to rest for 30 minutes, covered in foil, while you make the gravy. Pour the turkey juices from the tin into a jug, and skim 4 tablespoons of fat from the top into a saucepan. Skim off the rest of the fat from the juices and discard. Add the flour to the saucepan and whisk until blended. Pour in the port and stock and whisk until smooth and the gravy has thickened, then add the Worcestershire sauce and soy sauce. Bring to the boil, add the remaining turkey juices and season with salt and pepper. Pour the gravy into a warmed serving jug and serve with the turkey.

TIP
Use a wooden spoon or rubber spatula to help loosen the skin on the turkey crown. Insert the spoon end under the skin and push it around carefully, between the breast meat and skin, to get to the tricky bits your fingers can't reach.

Fish

For such a delicate taste and light texture nothing can beat fresh fish. While simple preparation is often all that's needed, some types of fish combine beautifully with different flavours and can be served in a huge variety of ways, either whole, or flaked and made into a mouth-watering pie or risotto (page 146).

Salmon, with its rich oily flesh, really holds its own as the centrepiece of a meal. I've included two of my favourite ways of serving it here: Salmon Fillets on a Bed of Spinach with Tarragon Sauce (page 130), a perfect dinner-party dish, and Potato Salad with Salmon and Tiger Prawns (page 128), which would be lovely served for a summer buffet.

Fish and salad come together again in the Lemon Sole with Fennel Slaw (page 132). Here I've used panko breadcrumbs for coating the fish. I find these are a really useful ingredient for the store cupboard as they give a particularly crisp, light-textured finish. The aniseed flavour of the fennel in this recipe provides a lovely, slightly unusual contrast to the delicate taste of the fish in a combination that I hope you'll enjoy as much as I do.

Generally speaking, fish needs to be cooked and served immediately, but there are some notable exceptions, fish pie being one of them (page 149). The recipe here offers a delicious variation on the classic dish with its crunchy 'soufflé crouton' topping – perfect for preparing in advance and guaranteed to go down a storm with a large gathering of family and friends. The Crab and Cod Fishcakes with Tomato Salsa (page 143) can also be made ahead, the fishcakes stored uncooked in the fridge, then fried shortly before serving. Served in smaller quantities, they would make a lovely first course.

POTATO SALAD WITH FRESH SALMON AND TIGER PRAWNS

THIS COLOURFUL SALAD is light yet substantial and with lots of lovely contrasting textures. Perfect for a summer buffet – just serve with green salad leaves.

SERVES 6–8

PREPARE AHEAD
The potato salad can be made a day in advance without the sliced radish and stored in the fridge, adding the radish, freshly cooked salmon and the prawns up to 4 hours ahead.

3 x 125g (4½ oz) middle-cut salmon fillets, skin on
½ lemon
16 cooked tiger prawns in their shells

FOR THE SALAD
500g (1lb 2oz) baby new potatoes
4 tbsp olive oil
3 tbsp Dijon mustard
1 tbsp caster sugar
3 tbsp white wine vinegar
6 tbsp mayonnaise
1 bunch of spring onions, finely sliced
150g (5oz) radishes, thinly sliced
4 celery sticks, finely diced
juice of ½ lemon
1 small bunch of parsley, chopped
salt and freshly ground black pepper

1 Preheat the oven to 180°C/160°C fan/Gas 4 and line a baking sheet with foil.

2 Put the potatoes in a saucepan, cover with water, season with salt and bring to the boil. Boil for about 15 minutes or until tender, then drain and slice each potato into quarters.

3 While the potatoes are cooking, arrange the salmon fillets, skin side down, on the prepared baking sheet, squeeze over the juice of half a lemon and season with salt and pepper. Cover with another sheet of foil, to make a parcel, and bake in the oven for about 15 minutes or until just cooked. Remove from the oven and leave to one side to cool, then remove the skin.

4 To make the salad, first mix the oil, mustard, sugar and vinegar together in a large bowl. Add the hot potatoes and season with salt and pepper, then stir to combine before setting aside to cool. Add the mayonnaise, spring onions, radishes and celery, mix together well and check the seasoning. Stir in the lemon juice.

5 Add half the chopped parsley to the potato salad, stirring to combine, and spoon the salad on to a large platter. Flake the salmon into large pieces and arrange on top, then sprinkle with the remaining parsley. Peel the shells from the tails of the prawns, leaving the heads on, and arrange in a line on top.

TIP
Adding the potato slices to the dressing while they're still warm allows the flavour to really soak into the potatoes.

Salmon fillets on a bed of spinach with tarragon sauce

An elegant dish that is quick and simple to prepare, this is perfect for a smart dinner party. If you wanted to get ahead to serve it for a gathering, season the fish and have it ready on a tray, and prepare the sauce and spinach in advance (see Prepare Ahead).

Serves 6

Prepare ahead
Although some preparation can be done in advance, this dish is best made and served immediately. The spinach can be cooked 1–2 hours before, and then fried to heat through before serving. The sauce can be made ahead of time, and kept refrigerated, then reheated over a gentle heat on the hob.

2 tbsp oil
50g (2oz) butter
6 middle-cut salmon fillets (about 150g/5oz each), skin on
700g (1½lb) baby spinach
salt and freshly ground black pepper

For the sauce
150ml (5fl oz) white wine
300ml (10fl oz) double cream
juice of ½ small lemon
a pinch of sugar
2 tsp finely chopped tarragon

1 Preheat the oven to 200°C/180°C fan/Gas 6.

2 Heat a large frying pan and add the oil and half the butter. Season the salmon fillets with salt and pepper and fry, skin side down, over a high heat for about 2 minutes until golden brown and crisp. Carefully turn over and fry for about another minute until lightly browned and sealed. Depending on the size of your pan, you may need to fry the salmon in batches.

3 Transfer the fillets to a baking tray, laying them skin side down, and pour over any oily juices from the frying pan. Slide the tray into the oven and roast for about 8 minutes or until just cooked through.

4 To make the sauce, pour the wine into a wide, shallow saucepan, bring to the boil and allow to bubble over a high heat to reduce by half. Add the cream and reduce further, stirring until slightly thickened, then add the lemon juice, sugar and tarragon and season with salt and pepper.

5 Put half the spinach into a colander, pour over enough boiling water to wilt it, then refresh in cold water, drain and squeeze out any liquid. Set aside and then repeat with the remaining spinach. It may seem like a lot of spinach, but don't worry – it wilts down to become more manageable once cooked.

6 Wipe out the frying pan and place back on the hob over a high heat, add the remaining butter and fry the spinach, stirring, for 1 minute, then season with salt and pepper.

7 Remove the skin from each salmon fillet. Spoon a pile of spinach on to each plate, sit a piece of salmon on top, pour over some of the sauce and serve hot.

LEMON SOLE WITH FENNEL SLAW

DELICATE SOLE PAIRED WITH FENNEL – two of my favourite ingredients! The panko breadcrumbs make a quick and crunchy coating for the lemon sole, while the fennel slaw provides a light and tangy contrast to the fish. Ask your fishmonger to skin the fillets, or follow the tip on page 150 to do it yourself.

SERVES 4

PREPARE AHEAD
The fish can be coated in breadcrumbs and chilled, covered in cling film, in the fridge for up to 24 hours before cooking. The fennel slaw can be prepared ahead, too, and kept, covered, in the fridge for 1–2 days.

FREEZE
The breaded fish can be frozen raw – defrost in the fridge before cooking.

plain flour, for coating
2 eggs
100g (4oz) panko breadcrumbs
4 lemon sole fillets (about 150g/5oz each), skinned
3 tbsp olive oil
a knob of butter
lemon slices, to serve

FOR THE SLAW
juice of ½ lemon
1 fennel bulb, trimmed
100ml (3½fl oz) full-fat crème fraîche
1 tbsp chopped parsley
salt and freshly ground black pepper

1   To make the fennel slaw, squeeze the lemon juice into a bowl. Slice the fennel in half through the root and remove the root entirely by cutting the wedge out. Then, using a mandolin or slicing very carefully with a knife, cut the fennel into very thin slices. Add to the lemon juice in the bowl, seasoning with salt and pepper. Stir in the crème fraîche and parsley and leave in the fridge for a minimum of 1 hour to soften.

2   Sprinkle a little flour on to a plate, beat the eggs in a shallow bowl and scatter the breadcrumbs over another plate. Season the lemon sole fillets with salt and pepper, then coat on both sides in the flour, dip in the beaten egg and coat in the breadcrumbs. Transfer to a separate plate and chill in the fridge, covered in cling film, if time allows.

3   Heat a large frying pan, add the oil and butter and fry the fish for about 2 minutes on each side until golden and crisp and cooked through. You may need to do this in batches. Remove the fish from the pan and drain on kitchen paper. Serve with a slice of lemon and a spoonful of slaw on the side.

Sea bass fillets with brown shrimp & caper sauce

Sea bass has a lovely creamy taste. I slightly prefer fillets to steaks as they are more delicate in flavour and texture.

Serves 6

Prepare ahead
The sauce, without the parsley, can be made 1 day ahead and reheated to serve with the freshly cooked fish.

3–4 tbsp plain flour, for coating
6 sea bass fillets (about 90g/3½oz each), skin on
a knob of butter
1 tbsp oil

For the sauce
a knob of butter
1 tbsp oil
1 small onion, finely chopped
200ml (7fl oz) white wine
300ml (10fl oz) double cream
2 tbsp chopped capers
juice of ½ small lemon
150g (5oz) cooked, peeled brown shrimps
2 tbsp chopped parsley
salt and freshly ground black pepper

1 To make the sauce, heat the butter and oil in a frying pan, add the onion and cook over a high heat for about 10 minutes until soft. Pour in the wine and boil to reduce by half, then add the cream and continue to boil, stirring all the while, until the sauce has thickened slightly. Stir in the capers, lemon juice and shrimps, season with a little salt and pepper to taste and keep warm until ready to serve.

2 Sprinkle the flour on a plate and season with salt and pepper. Coat the flesh side of each sea bass fillet in a thin layer of the seasoned flour, tapping off the excess.

3 Heat a large frying pan until very hot, add the butter and oil and fry the fillets, flesh side down, for 2 minutes until golden. Carefully turn the fillets over and fry for 2 minutes until the skin is crisp and the fish is cooked through. You may need to do this in batches of two fillets at a time in order not to crowd the pan.

4 To serve, stir the parsley into the shrimp and caper sauce, place a sea bass fillet, skin side down, on each plate and spoon over the sauce.

Prawn and ginger noodle stir-fry

Once all the ingredients are prepared, this can be cooked in no time, making it good to serve at the last minute. Present in individual bowls with some prawn crackers on the side.

Serves 4

Prepare ahead
The noodles can be cooked in advance and kept in the fridge, tossed with a little oil to stop them sticking. The vegetables can all be prepared ahead and stored in a freezer bag in the fridge.

150g (5oz) dried medium egg noodles
3 tbsp olive oil
2 large red peppers, deseeded and thinly sliced
1 red chilli, deseeded and finely chopped
8 spring onions, thinly sliced on the diagonal
100g (4oz) chestnut mushrooms, thickly sliced
3cm (1¼in) knob of fresh root ginger, grated (see tip on page 84)
225g (8oz) pak choi, thinly sliced, keeping white and green parts separate
350g (12oz) raw, peeled king prawns
salt and freshly ground black pepper

For the sauce
1 tbsp Chinese five-spice powder
3 tbsp soy sauce
3 tbsp runny honey
2 tsp white wine vinegar

To serve (optional)
4 pink radishes, thinly sliced
juice of ½ lemon
2 tbsp chopped coriander

1 Cook the noodles according to the packet instructions, drain and refresh in cold water.

2 Heat the oil in a large, non-stick frying pan or wok. Add the red peppers, chilli, spring onions, mushrooms, ginger and white parts of the pak choi, and fry over a high heat, stirring, for about 4 minutes until the vegetables are nearly cooked but still crisp.

3 Add the prawns and fry for a further minute or until starting to turn pink. Tip the drained noodles into the pan and add the green leaves of the pak choi, then fry for another minute or so, stirring to combine.

4 Mix the sauce ingredients together in a small bowl until smooth. Pour over the noodle mixture in the pan and season with salt and pepper, stirring continuously. Once the prawns are completely pink, transfer to individual plates or bowls to serve immediately. Garnish with the sliced radishes, squeeze over the lemon juice and scatter with the chopped coriander, if you like.

CRAB AND COD FISHCAKES WITH TOMATO SALSA

I HAVE NOT OVER-SPICED the fishcakes here as I don't want to mask the delicate flavour of the crabmeat. You can easily get cod loin of this size from a fishmonger, or simply use smaller cod fillets to make it up to the right weight. Also pictured overleaf.

MAKES 8 FISHCAKES/SERVES 4

PREPARE AHEAD
These can be made up into the shaped fishcakes and kept in the fridge for a day before frying.

FREEZE
The uncooked fishcakes can be frozen. Wrap each in cling film and put in a polythene bag. Defrost completely and fry as needed.

500g (1lb 2oz) floury potatoes (such as Désirée), peeled and diced
500g (1lb 2oz) cod loin, skinned
6 spring onions, finely chopped
2 tbsp full-fat mayonnaise
2 tsp Dijon mustard
1 x 130g (4½oz) dressed crab or 100g (4oz) mixed fresh crabmeat
2 tbsp chopped parsley
a dash of hot pepper sauce, such as Tabasco
50g (2oz) panko breadcrumbs
a knob of butter, plus extra for greasing
1 tbsp oil
salt and freshly ground black pepper

FOR THE SALSA
6 firm tomatoes, deseeded and cut into small dice
1 small (or ½) red onion, finely chopped
1 tbsp white wine vinegar
4 tbsp olive oil
2 tbsp chopped parsley

1 Preheat the oven to 200°C/180°C fan/Gas 6.

2 Put the potatoes into a saucepan of salted cold water. Bring to the boil and boil for about 15 minutes or until tender, then drain well, mash, seasoning with salt and pepper, and set aside to cool.

3 Grease a sheet of foil with butter, sit the cod loin in the centre, season with salt and pepper and wrap in the foil to make a parcel. Place on a baking sheet and cook for 20 minutes or until just cooked through. Set aside to cool down. When completely cool, carefully flake the fish into large pieces, reserving any cooking juices.

4 Spoon the cold mash into a bowl, mix in the spring onions, mayonnaise and mustard. Add 2 tablespoons of the fish cooking juice, then add the flaked cod and stir in the crabmeat. Add the parsley and hot pepper sauce and stir until combined, then taste for seasoning.

5 Shape the mixture into eight fishcakes, roughly 9cm (3½in) in diameter – you'll find it is easiest to do this with damp hands. Place on a tray and chill in the fridge for at least 15 minutes. Sprinkle the panko breadcrumbs on a plate and use to coat each fishcake. Return to the tray and chill again in the fridge for 30 minutes if time allows before frying.

6 To make the salsa, mix all the ingredients together and season with salt and pepper.

7 Heat a wide, heavy-based frying pan, add the butter and oil and fry the fishcakes over a high heat until golden all over, turning halfway through – about 4 minutes on each side. When frying, it's best not to overcrowd the pan: cook the fishcakes in two batches of four, if need be. Serve hot with the tomato salsa and a dressed salad.

Smoked haddock risotto

This kedgeree in the form of a risotto makes a lovely, hearty supper dish. I have used poached eggs, but you can substitute these with three hard-boiled eggs, if you prefer, cutting them into quarters to sit on top of each portion. This dish is best eaten as soon as it is made.

SERVES 6–8

500g (1lb 2oz) undyed smoked
    haddock fillet, skin on
1 bay leaf
8 black peppercorns
1 large leek, sliced, both green and
    white parts
3–4 tbsp chopped parsley, stalks
    reserved, plus extra to garnish
2 tbsp sunflower oil
2 garlic cloves, crushed
1 tbsp medium curry powder
350g (12oz) risotto rice
600ml (1 pint) hot fish stock
juice of ½ lemon
6 eggs (see tip overleaf)
salt and freshly ground black pepper

1 Place the haddock, skin side down, in a large, deep frying pan. Cover with 800ml (1 pint 8fl oz) of water, add the bay leaf, peppercorns, the white parts of the leek, and the reserved parsley stalks. Bring to the boil, cover with a lid and simmer gently for 5 minutes or until the haddock is cooked.

2 Lift out the haddock with a slotted spoon and transfer to a plate. Remove the skin and flake the fish into large pieces. Strain the liquid and reserve 750ml (1 pint 6fl oz) in a jug, discarding the other ingredients left in the sieve.

3 Heat the oil in a large, wide-based saucepan, add the green parts of the leek and fry over a medium heat for about 5 minutes. Add the garlic and fry for a minute, sprinkle in the curry powder and rice and fry over a high heat for a further minute, stirring so that the grains of rice are coated in the spice mixture.

4 Pour in the fish stock and reserved poaching liquid, season with salt and pepper and bring to the boil. Stir the mixture, cover with a lid and simmer, stirring occasionally, for 20–25 minutes until nearly all the liquid has been absorbed and the rice is soft and creamy. Add the lemon juice, chopped parsley leaves and the flaked haddock pieces.

5 To poach the eggs, crack each egg on to a small plate and gently slide into a pan of simmering water. Reduce the heat to low and swirl the water around the edges to give a neat shape to the poaching egg. Simmer for about 3 minutes or until the white is opaque. Lift out with a slotted spoon and drain, then place on a plate lined with kitchen paper to absorb any excess water and cover to keep warm. Repeat with the other eggs (see tip overleaf).

CONTINUED OVERLEAF

6 Divide the risotto between individual bowls and garnish with parsley. Serve each with a poached egg on top, opened slightly so the yolk runs.

TIPS

For the best results use the freshest eggs possible for poaching as the whites will be firmer.

To keep the eggs warm but without overcooking the yolks, which should be runny, place on a plate over a saucepan of hot water and cover with a dome of foil.

FISH PIE WITH SOUFFLÉ CROUTON TOPPING

THE CLASSIC FISH PIE has been given a delicious twist with a crunchy cheesy topping that perfectly offsets the smooth and creamy filling. It needs to be made slightly ahead as the filling is chilled in the fridge for an hour. Ask your fishmonger to skin the fish, or follow the tip overleaf for doing it yourself.

SERVES 6

PREPARE AHEAD
The filling can be made up to 8 hours ahead. Prepare the soufflé topping, assemble the dish and cook within an hour.

FOR THE FILLING
50g (2oz) butter, plus extra for greasing
1 leek, diced
50g (2oz) plain flour
600ml (1 pint) hot milk
2 tbsp chopped dill
2 tbsp lemon juice
350g (12oz) fresh haddock fillet, skinned and cut into even-sized cubes
350g (12oz) undyed smoked haddock fillet, skinned and cut into even-sized cubes
3 hard-boiled eggs, each cut into either 4 or 8 wedges
salt and freshly ground black pepper

FOR THE TOPPING
1 small (400g/14oz) loaf of white bread (2–3 days old)
50g (2oz) full-fat cream cheese
75g (3oz) butter
75g (3oz) mature Cheddar cheese, grated
1 large egg white

1   You will need a shallow 1.5-litre (2½-pint) ovenproof dish, approximately 30 x 20 x 6cm (12 x 8 x 2½in).

2   To make the filling for the pie, melt the butter in a saucepan, add the leek and gently soften over a low heat for 3–4 minutes until completely tender but not browned. Sprinkle in the flour and stir over a high heat for a minute. Gradually pour in the hot milk, whisking over a high heat until the sauce is smooth and thickened and has come to the boil.

3   Remove from the heat and add the chopped dill, lemon juice and cubes of fish and season with salt and pepper. Return to the heat and cook for 2 minutes, stirring, then remove from the hob and spoon into the ovenproof dish. Arrange the eggs on top of the sauce and press in gently. Level the top with the back of your spoon and set aside to cool. When cold, cover with cling film and chill in the fridge for about an hour or until firm.

4   Preheat the oven to 200°C/180°C fan/Gas 6 and grease the dish with a little melted butter.

5   To make the soufflé topping, remove the crusts from the loaf and cut into five slices, each about 1.5cm (⅝in) thick, and then into cubes; you will need to weigh out about 150g (5oz) of these croutons. Measure the cream cheese, butter and Cheddar into a saucepan and melt together over a low heat until runny. (The mixture may look curdled, but don't worry!) Remove from the heat and set the pan aside for a moment.

6   In a spotlessly clean bowl, whisk the egg white until stiff, then fold into the cheese mixture in the saucepan. Season with salt and pepper and carefully stir together, then stir in the croutons so they are fully coated in the mixture. Spoon on top of the fish filling so that the croutons form a single layer.

CONTINUED OVERLEAF

FISH PIE WITH SOUFFLÉ CROUTON TOPPING
CONTINUED

7 Bake in the oven for 25–30 minutes until golden and bubbling. If the dish starts getting too brown during cooking, simply cover with foil. Leave to stand for 5 minutes before serving with a salad or green vegetable.

TIPS

To skin the fish, place each one, skin side down, on a chopping board. Using a large, sharp knife, make a small cut about 1cm (½in) from the tail (or narrowest) end of the fillet. Cut through the flesh, but not through the tough skin. Now take the flap of skin firmly in one hand (a sprinkling of salt can help you grip the slippery fish). Angling the knife blade away from you at 45 degrees, insert it into the small cut and work it gently from side to side, cutting the flesh away from the skin in one piece. Discard the skin.

If the sauce is a little thick due to over-boiling, add a touch more milk to thin it down.

Vegetables
& Salads

VEGETABLES ARE WONDERFUL in that they can provide the focus for a meal or serve as a side to complement a main dish of meat or fish. And they can be served hot or cold, of course. In this chapter, I've brought together a range of recipes, from sustaining hot dishes like the Lentil Shepherd's Pie (page 174), an excellent vegetarian alternative to the meat-based classic, to summery salads packed with flavour, of which my current favourite must be the Watermelon, Feta, Cucumber and Mint Salad (page 165). My Butternut Squash and Lentil Samb (page 174) is a colourful and utterly scrumptious vegetable stew that would work as a main or a side dish and can easily be made in advance.

A vegetable dish doesn't have to be vegetarian, on the other hand, and there are a couple of delicious meat and veg combinations here: the Leek and Bacon Quiche (page 168), large enough to serve 8–12 people for lunch, and the Sprouts with Chestnuts and Pancetta (page 187), which would go to perfection with roast turkey (page 122) or chicken. Rather like a posh bubble and squeak, it would also be substantial enough to eat all on its own.

For a different take on another classic side dish, I would recommend the Celeriac and Potato Mash (page 184) – a very tasty alternative to the straight potato version and just as versatile. You'll find celeriac again, in the form of the more familiar Celeriac Remoulade, as one of six superb salads that I've grouped together for the Market Tapas recipes (pages 161–3). You could make them individually, if you liked, but I find they complement each other beautifully to make a whole mixed-salad meal in themselves.

Homemade condiments always go down well, if you can spare the time to make them, and I've included a couple of favourites here: Home-grown Chutney (page 178) – made with more or less any vegetables you have to hand and perfect for using up any gluts of seasonal home-grown produce – and a super-easy Fresh Cranberry Sauce (page 186). Served warm or cold, it is super-tasty too!

SUPERFOODS SALAD

THERE IS A WHOLE RANGE OF SUPERFOODS – foodstuffs that pack a real nutritional punch – and here is a salad using five of them in one dish: broccoli, garlic, beetroot, pumpkin seeds and olive oil. If you are unable to get fresh broad beans or peas, use frozen ones, add them to the pan of boiling water and cook for 1 minute, then add the broccoli and cook for a further minute so the beans/peas are boiled for 2 minutes in total.

SERVES 4–6

PREPARE AHEAD
The salad can be assembled without the beetroot up to 8 hours before serving to allow the flavours to develop. It can be kept, chilled in the fridge, for up to 24 hours. The dressing can be made in advance and stored in a sealed container in the fridge for 3–4 days.

350g (12oz) tenderstem broccoli, trimmed and cut into small, thin florets
100g (4oz) podded and skinned broad beans or peas
2 celery sticks, thinly sliced
2 cooked beetroot (60–75g/2½–3oz each), cut into batons (see tip)
25g (1oz) pumpkin seeds, toasted (see page 55)
salt and freshly ground black pepper

FOR THE DRESSING
2 garlic cloves, crushed
2 tbsp lemon juice
4 tbsp olive oil
1 tsp sugar

1 Bring a pan of salted water to the boil, add the broccoli and broad beans (or peas) and boil for 1 minute. Drain and refresh in cold water.

2 Tip the drained vegetables into a serving bowl and add the celery. Place the dressing ingredients in a separate, small bowl and mix until smooth. Pour into the serving bowl, season with salt and pepper and toss until the vegetables are well coated in the dressing. Add the beetroot batons and sprinkle with the toasted pumpkin seeds.

TIP
Use plastic gloves when preparing beetroot to avoid staining your hands. It's important to add at the very last stage of preparing the salad, as otherwise everything turns purple!

MARKET TAPAS <small>SERVES 6</small>

THESE ARE SIX OF MY FAVOURITE salad recipes. Once assembled, they can be served in individual bowls. Alternatively, you could serve a little of each on one plate to create a hearty mixed salad per person. Simply arrange the Caesar salad in the centre of a flat plate, with the other salads laid out in equal-sized piles around the salad in the middle. Serve with an interesting bread of your choice.

CAESAR SALAD

PREPARE AHEAD
The croutons can be made in advance and stored in an airtight container for 2 days. The dressing will keep for 2–3 days in a sealed container in the fridge.

2 slices of day-old white bread, crusts removed
3 tbsp olive oil
1 romaine lettuce heart, sliced
30g (1oz) Parmesan cheese, shaved
salt and freshly ground black pepper

FOR THE DRESSING
6 tbsp light mayonnaise
1½ tbsp Dijon mustard
2 tbsp grated Parmesan cheese
½ garlic clove, crushed
a few drops of Worcestershire sauce

1 Cut the bread into cubes, then add the olive oil to a non-stick frying pan, tip in the bread and fry over a high heat for 3–4 minutes until golden. Remove with a slotted spoon, transfer to a bowl and season with salt and pepper.

2 To make the dressing, measure all the ingredients into a separate bowl and beat together until smooth with 1–2 tablespoons of water. Toss the romaine lettuce in the dressing and scatter with the toasted croutons and grated Parmesan.

SUN-BLUSHED TOMATO AND FETA SALAD

PREPARE AHEAD
Once assembled, this keeps, covered, in the fridge for 1–2 days.

150g (5oz) sun-blushed tomatoes (see tip), snipped into quarters
75g (3oz) pitted black olives in oil, drained and halved
2 tbsp olive oil or oil drained from the sun-blushed tomatoes
150g (5oz) good-quality feta cheese, crumbled into small chunks

1 Place the tomatoes, olives and oil in a bowl and stir together, then gently mix in the feta.

TIP
If you would like to make your own 'sun'-blushed tomatoes, cut each one in half, arrange on a baking tray, sprinkle with salt and pepper and a little olive oil and cook at 75°C/55°C fan/Gas ¼ for about 6 hours.

CONTINUED OVERLEAF

CELERIAC REMOULADE

PREPARE AHEAD
The dressing can be made in advance and kept for 3–4 days in a sealed container in the fridge.

650g (1lb 7oz) celeriac, peeled and sliced into thin matchsticks (see tip)
juice of 1 lemon

FOR THE DRESSING
6 tbsp light mayonnaise
1 tbsp Dijon mustard
juice of ½ lemon
a pinch of sugar
salt and freshly ground black pepper

1   Put the celeriac in a bowl of about 100ml cold water and add the lemon juice. Toss well to prevent it going brown. To make the dressing, mix all the ingredients together and season with salt and pepper. Drain the celeriac, toss in the dressing and leave to soften for 30 minutes before serving.

TIP
For the best results, use a mandolin to slice the celeriac into matchsticks. However, if you're pressed for time, a food processor gives good results. Use the largest grating attachment to give a coarse grating, rather than matchsticks.

CARROT AND POPPYSEED SALAD

PREPARE AHEAD
The salad can be assembled and kept in the fridge for 2–3 days.

6 medium carrots, grated (see tip)
juice of 1 small lemon
4 tbsp olive oil
1 tsp caster sugar
1 tsp poppy seeds

1   Measure all the ingredients into a bowl, season with salt and pepper and mix well.

TIP
If time is limited, use a food processor to grate the carrots.

ROASTED RED PEPPER AND ARTICHOKE SALAD

PREPARE AHEAD
Once made, the salad can be stored, covered, in the fridge for 1–2 days.

300g (11oz) roasted red peppers in oil, drained and sliced
175g (6oz) chargrilled artichoke hearts in oil, drained and cut into pieces
2 tsp shredded basil leaves
2 tsp balsamic vinegar
salt and freshly ground black pepper

1 Mix the peppers and artichokes together in a bowl and season with salt and pepper. Add a little oil from the jar, if needed, along with the basil leaves and balsamic vinegar.

MIXED BEAN SALAD

PREPARE AHEAD
Assemble the salad and keep, covered, in the fridge for 2–3 days to help the flavours develop.

1 x 400g tin of mixed bean salad, drained and rinsed
2 spring onions, finely chopped
2 celery sticks, thinly sliced
1 large tomato, deseeded and finely diced
salt and freshly ground black pepper

FOR THE DRESSING
3 tbsp olive oil
1 tbsp white wine vinegar
1 tsp sugar
2 tsp Dijon mustard
1 tbsp chopped tarragon
1 tbsp chopped parsley

1 Put all the salad ingredients in a bowl. Mix the dressing ingredients in a separate bowl or jug, pour over the salad, season well with salt and pepper and toss together.

WATERMELON, FETA, CUCUMBER AND MINT SALAD

THIS IS MY FAVOURITE SALAD at the moment – fresh, full of flavour and crunchy texture. Any small black seeds left in the watermelon after deseeding can be eaten, although I prefer to remove the larger ones. This delicious salad is best made and served on the same day.

Serves 6 as a main dish or 10–12 as part of a buffet

½ cucumber
½ small watermelon, peeled, deseeded and cut into 2cm (¾in) cubes
200g (7oz) good-quality feta cheese, crumbled into small cubes
50g (2oz) pitted black olives in oil, halved
1 small bunch of mint, chopped

For the dressing
4 tbsp olive oil (or oil reserved from the olives)
juice of ½ lemon
salt and freshly ground black pepper

1 Peel the cucumber with a potato peeler, cut in half lengthways and, using a teaspoon, scoop out and discard the seeds. Cut into crescent shapes.

2 Layer half the watermelon, cucumber, feta and olives in a bowl, repeat again, then sprinkle with the chopped mint. For the dressing, whisk together the oil and lemon juice, season with salt and pepper and pour into the bowl. Serve chilled.

Leek and bacon quiche

A CLASSIC RECIPE but with a twist from the added leeks and layer of mustard, this makes a large quiche that's full of flavour and delicious, melting texture. For a crisp base, it's always best to cook the pastry case first before adding the filling.

SERVES 8–12

PREPARE AHEAD
Once cooked, this quiche will keep for 1–2 days in the fridge.

FREEZE
This can be frozen, but for best results defrost slowly in the fridge so the filling retains its texture. Reheat and serve warm.

FOR THE PASTRY
225g (8oz) plain flour, plus extra for dusting
150g (5oz) cold butter, cubed
1 egg, beaten

FOR THE FILLING
a knob of butter
2 medium leeks, roughly chopped
350g (12oz) unsmoked streaky bacon, snipped into small pieces
2 tbsp Dijon mustard
175g (6oz) Gruyère cheese, grated
6 eggs
600ml (1 pint) double cream
2 heaped tbsp chopped parsley
salt and freshly ground black pepper

1 You will need a 28cm (11in) round, loose-bottomed tart tin or fluted ceramic flan dish and some baking beans (see tip overleaf). Preheat the oven to 200°C/180°C fan/Gas 6.

2 To make the pastry, measure the flour and butter into a food processer and whizz until the mixture resembles breadcrumbs (or place in a mixing bowl and rub the butter into the flour with your fingertips). Add the egg and 1 tablespoon of water and mix again. Add more water if needed and mix into a smooth dough.

3 Lightly dust a work surface with flour and roll out the dough into a circle large enough to line the tart tin or dish and about 3mm (⅛in) thick. Press into the base and sides of the tin and make a small lip around the top. Prick the base all over with a fork and place in the fridge to chill for 15 minutes.

4 Line the chilled pastry case with greaseproof paper and fill with baking beans. Bake in the oven for 15–20 minutes, then remove the beans and paper, lower the temperature to 160°C/140°C fan/Gas 3 and return the pastry case to the oven to dry out for 5–10 minutes. Remove from the oven and set aside to cool. Increase the temperature to 190°C/170°C fan/Gas 5.

5 Meanwhile, make the filling. Melt the butter in a frying pan, add the leeks and bacon and fry over a high heat for about 15 minutes. Lower the heat, cover with a lid and cook gently for about 10 minutes until softened. Remove the lid and fry over a high heat – stirring frequently to stop the cooked leeks from catching and burning – to drive off any liquid and crisp up the bacon. Leave to cool a little.

6 Spread the mustard over the base of the cooked pastry case with the back of a spoon and then spoon in the bacon and leek mixture. Season with salt and pepper and add half the cheese.

CONTINUED OVERLEAF

7 Crack the eggs into a large bowl and add the cream and parsley, then season with salt and pepper and whisk by hand to combine. Pour the mixture into the tart case (see tip) and sprinkle over the remaining cheese.

8 Bake in the oven for 30–35 minutes until golden brown and just set. Serve warm with a fresh salad.

TIPS

If you do not have baking beans, you can use pasta, dried pulses, or uncooked rice from your store cupboard to fill the case before baking.

To fill the quiche without spillages, pour half the egg mixture into the case, then place the tin on the oven shelf, near the front, ready for baking. Pour in the remaining egg mix while the quiche is in situ on the shelf, and sprinkle over the cheese. Then carefully slide it further into the oven and close the door.

ONION, COURGETTE AND BLUE CHEESE PUFF TARTS

THESE DELICIOUS CHEESY SQUARES are perfect for a summer lunch with salad or for a light supper. Once you have tried them, you could experiment with different toppings, to your own taste. Some walnuts may be tasty with the Stilton, for instance, or you could use any strong cheese left over in the fridge. For a milder flavour, try mozzarella or a mild Cheddar.

MAKES 6 TARTS

PREPARE AHEAD
These can be assembled and kept in the fridge for up to 8 hours, then cooked in the oven to serve.

1 x 320g packet of ready-rolled, all-butter puff pastry
plain flour, for dusting
a knob of butter
2 tbsp olive oil
2 large onions, thinly sliced
1 tbsp light muscovado sugar
2 tsp balsamic vinegar
2 large courgettes, sliced on the diagonal
3 tomatoes, deseeded and sliced into thin strips
200g (7oz) Stilton, crumbled into small cubes
1 egg, beaten
salt and freshly ground black pepper

1 Preheat the oven to 220°C/200°C fan/Gas 7 and line a baking sheet or tray with baking paper.

2 Lay the pastry on a floured work surface and re-roll a little more, to a rectangle measuring 30 x 45cm (12 x 18in). Using a sharp knife, halve the dough widthways and then cut each half into three 15cm (6in) squares. Use the knife to score a border around each square, about 2cm (¾in) in from the edge. Prick the base of the inside square with a fork and place on the prepared baking sheet.

3 Heat the butter and 1 tablespoon of the oil in a large frying pan, add the onions and fry gently for about 10 minutes to soften. Stir in the sugar and balsamic vinegar, cover with a lid and cook over a low heat for about 15 minutes until completely soft. Remove the lid, drive off any liquid over a high heat, stirring continuously, until golden and lightly caramelised. Season with salt and pepper, then remove with a slotted spoon and set aside to cool.

4 Add the remaining oil to the pan and fry the courgettes over a high heat for about 2 minutes on each side until golden. You may have to do this in batches so as not to overcrowd the pan.

5 Spread the caramelised onion and courgettes over the pastry squares. Arrange the tomato slices on top and scatter with the cubes of cheese. Brush the beaten egg around the pastry border and bake in the oven for 20–25 minutes or until golden brown and crisp. Serve hot or warm with dressed salad leaves.

LENTIL SHEPHERD'S PIE

THIS IS A VEGETARIAN VERSION of a classic shepherd's pie. The lentils make a delicious, slightly nutty, substitute for the usual minced lamb.

SERVES 6–8

PREPARE AHEAD
This dish can be assembled up to 12 hours beforehand and left to cool down completely, then cooked in the oven, preheated to 200°C/180°C fan/Gas 6, for 30–40 minutes.

FREEZE
Cool the assembled pie, then cover and freeze or divide into smaller portions and store in freezer containers. Defrost fully and cook in the oven for 30–35 minutes until piping hot and golden.

2 tbsp olive oil
2 onions, chopped
3 garlic cloves, crushed
2 x 400g tins of chopped tomatoes
600ml (1 pint) vegetable stock
250g (9oz) dried Puy lentils, rinsed
2 tbsp tomato purée
1–2 tbsp Worcestershire sauce
250g (9oz) spinach, any large leaves torn into smaller pieces
300g (11oz) large chestnut mushrooms, thickly sliced
salt and freshly ground black pepper

FOR THE TOPPING
1.2kg (2lb 10oz) large floury potatoes (such as King Edward), peeled and cubed
a knob of butter
3–4 tbsp milk
100g (4oz) mature Cheddar cheese, grated

1 You will need a 2-litre (3½-pint) ovenproof dish.

2 Heat the oil in a large, deep frying pan, add the onions and garlic and fry over a high heat for 3–4 minutes. Add the chopped tomatoes with the stock, lentils, tomato purée and Worcestershire sauce and bring to the boil. Cover with a lid and simmer over a low heat for 1–1¼ hours until the lentils are tender. Only once the lentils are tender, season with salt and pepper.

3 Add the spinach and mushrooms and stir over the heat until the spinach has wilted and the mushrooms are cooked. Tip into the ovenproof dish and set aside to cool.

4 Cook the potatoes in a pan of boiling, salted water for 15–20 minutes until tender. Drain and return to the pan, add the butter and milk and mash until smooth, seasoning with salt and pepper.

5 Meanwhile, preheat the oven to 200°C/180°C fan/Gas 6.

6 Spoon the mashed potato on top of the lentil mixture and sprinkle with the grated cheese, then bake in the oven – placed on a baking tray in case any of the mixture bubbles over during cooking – for 30–35 minutes or until golden and bubbling.

Butternut squash and lentil samb

Inspired by the south Indian sambar, or lentil-based vegetable stew, this colourful dish is lovely served warm with chops or fish, or on its own with bread. It can also be eaten cold as a salad.

Serves 6 as a main dish or 12 as a side dish

Prepare ahead
This can be made up to a day ahead, kept in a covered container in the fridge and reheated.

4 tbsp olive oil
2 large onions, chopped
1 leek, sliced
5 garlic cloves, crushed
1 red pepper, deseeded and diced
250g (9oz) dried Puy lentils, rinsed
100ml (3½fl oz) white wine
600ml (1 pint) chicken or vegetable
    stock
1 large butternut squash (about
    800g/1¾lb), peeled, deseeded and
    cut into 2cm (¾in) chunks
1 tbsp Dijon mustard
3 tbsp chopped parsley
salt and freshly ground black pepper

1 Preheat the oven to 220°C/200°C fan/Gas 7.

2 Heat 2 tablespoons of the oil in a deep frying pan, add the onions, leek, garlic and red pepper and fry over a medium-high heat for 5 minutes until starting to soften. Stir in the lentils (see tip), pour in the white wine and stock and bring to the boil, stirring. Cover with a lid, lower the heat and simmer for 40–45 minutes or until the lentils are tender. Remove the lid for the last 5–10 minutes if there is still a lot of liquid.

3 Meanwhile, pour the remaining oil into a large roasting tin, add the squash, tossing to coat in the oil, and season with salt and pepper. Roast in the oven for 25–30 minutes or until golden and tender.

4 Add the squash to the lentils, season with salt and pepper, stir in the mustard and parsley and serve hot.

TIP
Do not season the lentils before they are cooked as this will make the outer skins tough.

Home-grown chutney

THERE'S NOTHING NICER than making chutney from your own, home-grown vegetables; I have added a little spice too. Once bottled, it's best to leave the chutney for at least a month in a cool dark place for the flavour to mature. It can be stored like this, unopened, for between six months and a year. Also pictured overleaf.

MAKES ABOUT 2KG (4LB 6OZ)

900g (2lb) tomatoes, skinned (see tip) and chopped
750g (1lb 10oz) onions, chopped fairly small
1 large aubergine, 1 courgette and 3 red peppers, roughly chopped (about 900g/2lb prepared weight)
4 fat garlic cloves, crushed
1 tbsp grated fresh root ginger (see tip on page 84)
1 large red chilli, deseeded and chopped
350g (12oz) granulated sugar
300ml (10fl oz) distilled malt vinegar
1 tbsp salt
1 tbsp mustard seeds, crushed
1 tbsp paprika

1 Put all the prepared vegetables into a large preserving pan with the garlic, ginger and chilli and gradually bring to the boil to allow the vegetables to release their juices. Cover with a lid, lower the heat and gently simmer for about an hour, stirring from time to time, until the vegetables are tender.

2 Add the remaining ingredients and bring to the boil, stirring until the sugar has dissolved. Continue boiling with the lid off for up to 30 minutes until the mixture has a chunky, thick consistency and any surplus liquid has evaporated. Take care at the end of the cooking time to stir so that the chutney doesn't catch on the bottom of the pan.

3 Ladle into sterilised jars (see tip). Using a jam funnel makes this process a lot easier. Cover with screw-top lids and seal while hot.

TIPS
To skin the tomatoes, make a cross in the top of each one using a sharp knife, immerse in boiling water for a couple of minutes, then plunge in cold water and drain. The skin should peel off easily.

To sterilise the jars, first wash them and the lids in soapy water. Rinse but don't dry, then leave in the oven, preheated to 150°C/130°C fan/Gas 2, for 10 minutes. Fill the jars with the chutney while they are still warm. Alternatively, wash the jars in the dishwasher and use straight away.

Potato wedges

These are a great alternative to chips or jacket potatoes and are so quick to prepare. If you want to be really healthy, simply roast them without the oil. These are best cooked and served immediately.

Serves 4 as a side dish

2 large firm potatoes (such as King
    Edward), unpeeled
1 tbsp olive oil
a little paprika
coarse sea salt and freshly ground
    black pepper
soured cream, to serve (optional)

1 Preheat the oven to 200°C/180°C fan/Gas 6 and slide a baking tray into the oven to get hot.

2 Wash and dry the potatoes but leave the skin on. Cut each potato in half lengthways and then each half into thin wedges, about 1cm (½in) thick.

3 Toss the wedges in the olive oil and paprika. Lay a piece of non-stick baking paper on the hot baking tray and arrange the wedges flat in a single layer. If there are too many wedges to fit on one tray in a single layer, overflow to a second tray – it is important not to overfill the trays or the wedges won't crisp.

4 Grind over some black pepper and roast for about 20 minutes, turning the wedges halfway through cooking, until golden brown. Sprinkle with coarse sea salt and serve immediately with soured cream, if you like.

ASIAN SLAW

A HEALTHY VERSION OF COLESLAW with a sweet chilli, sesame and mustard dressing instead of the more usual mayonnaise, this is best made a day or two ahead for the flavours to infuse and the vegetables to soften slightly. To save time, you could use a food processor to cut up the vegetables rather than doing it all by hand. It would make a delicious accompaniment to the Chilli Burgers on page 77.

SERVES 6 AS A SIDE DISH

PREPARE AHEAD
This can be kept in the fridge, covered, for 2–3 days. For the best flavour, remove from the fridge 1–2 hours before serving to bring up to room temperature.

350g (12oz) white cabbage, finely shredded
1 large carrot, cut into matchsticks
200g (7oz) red radishes, thinly sliced
6 spring onions, sliced
1 bunch of coriander, roughly chopped
50g (2oz) sesame seeds, toasted
salt and freshly ground black pepper

FOR THE DRESSING
2 tbsp Dijon mustard
3 tbsp white wine vinegar
4 tbsp sweet chilli sauce
4 tbsp olive oil
2 tbsp sesame oil
1 tsp sugar

1 Place the cabbage, carrot, radishes, spring onions and chopped coriander in a large bowl and season with salt and pepper.

2 Mix the dressing ingredients together in a small bowl and pour over the salad. Toss together so that the vegetables are well coated in the dressing and leave in the fridge for a few hours or preferably overnight.

3 Arrange in a bowl or on a platter and scatter with the toasted sesame seeds to serve.

CHRISTMAS SIDES

EACH SERVES 6–8 AS A SIDE DISH

PERFECT TO SERVE WITH CHRISTMAS LUNCH or over the festive period, these are some of my favourite winter side dishes, and make the perfect foil to roast turkey and stewed game, such as the Turkey Crown with Orange (page 122) and Venison Casserole with Cherry and Red Wine Sauce (page 117).

CELERIAC AND POTATO MASH

PREPARE AHEAD
This can be made up to 2 days ahead and kept in the fridge.

1kg (2lb 3oz) floury potatoes (such as King Edward), peeled and cut into cubes
a knob of butter
2 large celeriac (about 1kg/2lb 3oz), peeled and cut into cubes
200ml (7fl oz) full-fat crème fraîche
salt and freshly ground black pepper

THIS IS SUCH A DELICIOUS COMBINATION and a nice change from plain mashed potato – just make sure to season it well. It would make a great side dish to serve with meat or fish, or even your Christmas turkey.

1   Put the potatoes in a large saucepan, cover with cold water, add salt and bring to the boil, then boil for about 15 minutes or until tender. Drain and mash or put through a potato ricer, add the butter and season with salt and pepper.

2   While the potatoes are boiling, put the celeriac in another saucepan, cover with cold, salted water and bring to the boil, then boil for about 15 minutes or until tender. Drain and whizz into a purée using a hand blender or food processor, then stir in the crème fraîche. Add the celeriac to the potato, check the seasoning and mix to combine.

TIP
I like to use King Edward potatoes for a really good mash.

RED CABBAGE

PREPARE AHEAD
Can be made up to 2 days ahead and
reheated gently in a low oven.

1 large red cabbage (about 1kg/
   2lb 3oz)
1 medium leek, finely sliced
450g (1lb) cooking apples, peeled
   and roughly chopped
5 tbsp cranberry sauce from a jar
2 tbsp white or red wine vinegar or
   cider vinegar
50g (2oz) butter
a pinch of sugar (optional)
salt and freshly ground black pepper

THIS IS A LOVELY SAVOURY DISH, the cabbage still retaining its
texture, while the leek, apples and other flavourings melt into it.

1   Preheat the oven to 150°C/130°C fan/Gas 2.

2   Peel off and discard any dry outer leaves from the cabbage.
   Cut the cabbage in half, removing the core, and slice thinly.
   Arrange a little cabbage over the base of a large ovenproof
   saucepan or sauté pan. Add the sliced leek and chopped
   apples in layers with the cranberry sauce and the rest of
   the cabbage. Season lightly with salt and pepper as you go,
   then pour over the vinegar and dot with the butter.

3   Cover with a lid and bring to the boil over a high heat.
   When the cabbage is hot and the butter has melted, transfer
   to the oven to bake for 2–2½ hours, stirring occasionally,
   until tender – the red cabbage should be dark and rich
   in colour, as well as soft and glossy. Check the seasoning,
   adding a little sugar if overly sharp, and serve hot.

FRESH CRANBERRY SAUCE

PREPARE AHEAD
The sauce can be made up to
1 day ahead and kept, covered,
in the fridge.

225g (8oz) fresh cranberries
150g (5oz) caster sugar
1 small, thin-skinned orange, cut
   into quarters, seeds removed
½ tsp mixed spice powder
   a pinch of freshly grated nutmeg

A FRESH SAUCE made with raw cranberries, this is very different from the bought variety in a jar and with a distinctively homemade taste. My family love it! Served cold, it would go beautifully with cold meats.

1 Place all the ingredients in a food processor and whizz until smooth. Serve cold or gently heat to serve warm.

SPROUTS WITH CHESTNUTS AND PANCETTA

PREPARE AHEAD

The sprouts can be cooked on the morning of the day you want to serve them. Cook for 3 minutes and leave at room temperature, to add to the cooked chestnuts and onions.

900g (2lb) small sprouts
50g (2oz) butter
200g (7oz) thinly sliced pancetta, cut into small pieces
1 onion, finely chopped
225g (8oz) frozen chestnuts, defrosted and halved
salt and freshly ground black pepper

THESE MAKE a lovely alternative to boiled or steamed sprouts for Christmas. They are best eaten freshly cooked, but any leftovers can be stored in the fridge for a day.

1 Remove the outer leaves from the sprouts, trim the base of each one and cut in half lengthways. Cook the prepared sprouts in boiling salted water for 4–5 minutes or until nearly tender. Drain and refresh in cold water to set the bright green colour.

2 Melt half the butter in a large frying pan and fry the pancetta for 3–4 minutes until crispy, then remove from the pan with a slotted spoon. Add the remaining butter with the onion and chestnuts and fry for around 10 minutes until the onion is soft. Stir in the pancetta and sprouts, season with pepper and serve piping hot.

TIP
If you are cooking the sprouts ahead of time, ensure that they are at room temperature when you add them to the pan. If they are added straight from the fridge, they take too long to heat through.

Pasta
& Rice

No store cupboard is complete without pasta in various shapes and sizes or long- and short-grain rice, and this section brings together some of my favourite ways of preparing them.

Pasta must be the ultimate comfort food, especially when made into an all-in-one dish, and I've included three such recipes here – perfect for serving the family for an informal meal. The Saturday Night Pasta (page 198) and Garlic Mushroom Penne Gratin (page 208) each combine penne (though any comparable pasta shape would do) with a delicious mixture of ingredients, which is then sprinkled with cheese and cooked in the oven or under the grill until bubbling and golden. Impossible to resist!

The Lasagne Express (page 201) offers a speedier and rather different way of making the classic dish, using crème fraîche instead of the usual béchamel sauce and a gorgeous combination of pork sausage meat, chestnut mushrooms and spinach. Like the other two pasta dishes, it can be made up to a day ahead or popped in the freezer for serving at a later date. My family just love this lasagne.

For the most delicious way to present basmati rice, why not try cooking it in the Iranian style? The recipe for Persian Rice (page 194) provides instructions for preparing the rice with spices and other ingredients and then steaming it through a layer of scrunched-up baking paper to produce extraordinarily soft and fluffy grains with a wonderfully buttery crust.

The lightly spiced Malay Fried Rice (page 197) offers something a bit different for a week-night supper, while the ideal dish for sharing must be paella (page 207) with its winning mixture of rich, tangy rice with prawns, mussels and tender pieces of chicken.

PERSIAN RICE

HERE BASMATI RICE is cooked in the traditional Iranian way: the holes made in the rice allowing steam to pass between the grains and the scrunched-up baking paper, producing a wonderfully subtle-tasting dish with a soft fluffy texture. It is ideal paired with the Harissa Spiced Lamb on page 84.

SERVES 6 AS A SIDE DISH

PREPARE AHEAD
The rice can be cooked until steaming, then cooled quickly and stored in the fridge for a maximum of 24 hours. (It's important to cool the rice quickly.) Place in an ovenproof dish, cover with foil and reheat in the oven at a medium temperature for 20 minutes or until piping hot.

100g (4oz) ready-to-eat dried
  apricots, snipped into strips
¼ tsp saffron strands
200ml (7fl oz) boiling water
300g (11oz) basmati rice, rinsed
2 tbsp olive oil
50g (2oz) butter
1 large onion, chopped
1 tsp cardamon pods (about 15),
  husks removed and seeds crushed
1 tsp ground cumin seeds
juice and finely grated zest of
  1 orange
2 large carrots, coarsely grated
1 cinnamon stick
salt and freshly ground black pepper

1 Place the apricot strips and saffron strands in a heatproof bowl and pour over the boiling water. Set aside for 30 minutes for the apricots to plump up.

2 Meanwhile, measure the rice into a separate bowl, cover with cold water and leave to soak for 30 minutes. Once soaked, boil in a pan of fresh water for about 3 minutes, then drain.

3 Heat the oil and butter in a heavy-based, non-stick sauté pan. Add the onion and ground spices and fry for about 10 minutes until golden. Add the boiled rice, the apricots and saffron with the soaking liquid, and the orange juice, carrots and cinnamon stick. Season with salt and pepper and stir over a high heat to combine.

4 Make six holes in the rice, using the handle of a wooden spoon. Cover the surface of the rice with damp crumpled baking paper and sit a lid on top.

5 Cook over a low heat, without stirring, for 35–40 minutes. Increase the heat to medium-high for 5–10 minutes or until a buttery golden crust is created on the bottom of the pan. Spoon out the rice on to a warm platter, then, using a fish slice, loosen the crust to turn it out in one piece so that the crispy base is now on top. Alternatively, loosen the rice crust with the fish slice, then place a warm serving platter over the saucepan and turn out so that the crispy base is now on top.

6 Garnish with the orange zest and cinnamon stick and serve warm or cold, removing the cinnamon stick before eating.

MALAY FRIED RICE

THIS IS A REALLY TASTY DISH and only lightly spiced, which makes it ideal for those with a preference for milder dishes. Perfect for a quick supper, it can be made and served immediately or the basic recipe can be made up in advance and the eggs fried when you're ready to serve.

SERVES 6

PREPARE AHEAD
This dish, minus the fried eggs, can be stored in the fridge for up to 1 day and heated through thoroughly to serve. Be sure to cool the rice quickly before chilling.

FREEZE
The rice freezes well without the fried egg topping.

250g (9oz) long-grain rice
150g (5oz) frozen petits pois
5 tbsp oil, plus extra for the eggs
2 skinless, boneless chicken breasts, sliced into strips roughly the size of your little finger
1 tbsp runny honey
2 large onions, roughly chopped
3 garlic cloves, crushed
1 red pepper, deseeded and cut into 1cm (½in) dice
200g (7oz) button mushrooms, sliced
½ tsp medium chilli powder
1 tbsp medium curry powder
4 tbsp soy sauce, plus extra to serve
6 eggs
salt and freshly ground black pepper

1 Tip the rice into a pan of boiling, salted water and boil according to the packet instructions, adding the frozen peas 3 minutes before the end of cooking. Drain well and set aside.

2 Heat 1 tablespoon of the oil in a large frying pan or wok. Add the chicken strips and season with salt and pepper. Drizzle in the honey and toss over a high heat for 4–5 minutes or until the chicken is golden all over and cooked through. Remove from the pan and set aside.

3 Pour the remaining oil into the same frying pan, add the onions, garlic and red pepper and fry over a high heat for 4–5 minutes, stirring occasionally. Add the mushrooms and spices, stirring well to combine, and fry for a further minute. Tip in the cooked rice and peas, add the chicken strips and soy sauce and toss together over a high heat, seasoning to taste with salt and pepper.

4 Heat a little oil in a large, non-stick frying pan and fry the eggs until the whites are set.

5 Divide the chicken and rice between plates, placing one fried egg on top of each portion. Sprinkle the eggs with salt and pepper to taste and serve with extra soy sauce if you like.

Saturday night pasta

A WONDERFULLY COMFORTING DISH, this can be made ahead and will go down really well with the family. It is certainly my grandchildren's favourite! I've used penne in this dish but any similar pasta shape would do, such as fusilli or orecchiette.

SERVES 6–8

PREPARE AHEAD
The pasta can be cooked up to 24 hours ahead, following the instructions in step 2, then kept in the fridge. The dish can be assembled fully and chilled overnight in the fridge, then cooked at 200°C/180°C fan/Gas 6 for 30 minutes.

butter, for greasing
250g (9oz) dried penne
1 onion, roughly chopped
3 skinless, boneless chicken breasts, cut into thin strips roughly the size of your little finger
1 tbsp paprika
1 tbsp olive oil
salt and freshly ground black pepper

FOR THE SAUCE
50g (2oz) butter
50g (2oz) plain flour
750ml (1 pint 6fl oz) hot milk (see tip)
1 tsp Dijon mustard
100g (4oz) Parmesan cheese, coarsely grated
2 large tomatoes, deseeded and cut into small cubes

1 You will need a shallow 1.75-litre (3-pint) ovenproof dish. Preheat the oven to 220°C/200°C fan/Gas 7 and butter the dish.

2 Cook the penne with the onion in boiling, salted water according to the packet instructions. Drain, refresh in cold water and leave to drain again in the colander.

3 Put the chicken strips in a resealable freezer bag with the paprika and a little salt and pepper, seal the bag and shake to coat. Heat the oil in a large frying pan and quickly fry the chicken over a high heat for about 2 minutes until golden and just cooked through (you may need to do this in batches). Using a slotted spoon, transfer the fried chicken to a plate and set aside.

4 To make the sauce, melt the butter in a large saucepan, add the flour and whisk together to form a roux. Cook for 1 minute, then gradually add the hot milk, whisking over a high heat until the sauce is smooth and thickened, and allow to boil for 4 minutes. Stir in the mustard and half the cheese and season with salt and pepper.

5 Add the pasta and onion to the sauce in the pan and stir together. Spoon half this mixture into the dish, arrange the chicken strips over the top and spoon the remaining pasta and sauce on top of the chicken. Scatter over the tomatoes and then top with the remaining cheese. Bake in the oven for about 20 minutes until piping hot and golden.

TIP
To save an extra pan, pour the milk into a microwave-proof jug and heat in a microwave on high for 1–2 minutes.

LASAGNE EXPRESS

THIS MAKES A REAL CHANGE from classic lasagne and is so much quicker: no béchamel sauce, just crème fraîche, and the tomato sauce is not cooked beforehand. Lasagne sheets can vary in size, so you may need more or fewer sheets – you need enough for two layers of pasta to fit the dish. Soaking the sheets of dried lasagne really helps to soften them so that they absorb the sauce better. You could also use fresh sheets of lasagne, in place of dried.

SERVES 6

PREPARE AHEAD
The lasagne can be prepared up to 1 day in advance and cooked when required; this helps the pasta to soften further, allowing the sauce to be absorbed. Once cooked, the lasagne can be kept in the fridge for 1–2 days.

FREEZE
The uncooked dish can be frozen. Defrost fully before cooking.

butter, for greasing
about 6 large dried, no pre-cook
  lasagne sheets
75g (3oz) mature Cheddar cheese,
  grated

FOR THE PORK AND SPINACH SAUCE
1 tbsp oil
450g (1lb) pork sausage meat
1 tbsp plain flour
1 red chilli, deseeded and finely
  chopped
2 fat garlic cloves, crushed
250g (9oz) chestnut mushrooms, sliced
200ml (7fl oz) full-fat crème fraîche
100g (4oz) baby spinach, roughly
  chopped
salt and freshly ground black pepper

FOR THE TOMATO SAUCE
500g (1lb 2oz) passata
2 tbsp sun-dried tomato paste
1 tsp light muscovado sugar
1 tbsp chopped thyme leaves
1 tbsp chopped sage

1 You will need a shallow 2.25-litre (4-pint) ovenproof dish measuring about 30 x 20 x 6cm (12 x 8 x 2½in). Preheat the oven to 200°C/180°C fan/Gas 6 and butter the dish.

2 Soak the lasagne sheets in recently boiled warm water to soften while you prepare the two sauces.

3 Heat the oil in a large, non-stick frying pan, add the sausage meat and brown over a high heat for 5–10 minutes until golden, breaking up the meat with two wooden spoons. Sprinkle in the flour and fry for a minute, then add the chilli, garlic and mushrooms and fry for about 5 minutes. Stir in the crème fraîche and spinach, bring to the boil and allow to bubble for a couple of minutes. Season well with salt and pepper and set aside.

4 To make the tomato sauce, mix all the ingredients together in a jug or bowl and season well with salt and pepper. Drain the lasagne sheets ready for assembling.

5 Divide the pork and spinach sauce into three and spoon one-third into the base of the ovenproof dish. Spoon one-third of the tomato sauce on top and arrange half the pasta sheets over the tomato sauce. Repeat using two more layers of pork and spinach and tomato sauce and one of pasta. Sprinkle over the grated cheese.

6 Bake in the oven for 30–35 minutes or until the pasta is tender and the top of the dish is golden brown and bubbling around the edges.

Seafood linguine with fresh tomato sauce

This recipe tastes of the sea – full of flavour and healthy too. It is best made and eaten on the same day. You can replace the clams with the same weight of mussels, if you prefer. Also pictured overleaf.

Serves 6

250g (9oz) dried linguine
3 tbsp olive oil
3 banana shallots, thinly sliced
1 red chilli, deseeded and finely
  chopped
2 garlic cloves, crushed
500g (1lb 2oz) fresh live clams,
  scrubbed (see tip)
250ml (9fl oz) white wine
juice of ½ lemon
25g (1oz) butter
6 large king scallops, each sliced in
  half horizontally
150g (5oz) prepared squid, sliced
  into pieces or rings
150g (5oz) raw, peeled king prawns
5 large tomatoes, deseeded and diced
salt and freshly ground black pepper
4 tbsp chopped parsley, to garnish

1 Cook the linguine in boiling, salted water according to the packet instructions, drain and set aside.

2 Heat the oil in a large, deep frying pan, add the shallots, chilli and garlic and fry over a high heat for a couple of minutes, then add the clams and fry for a further 5 minutes.

3 Pour in the wine and lemon juice, cover with a lid and cook for 3–4 minutes until the clams are open (discard any that have not opened). Stir in the drained linguine, season with a little salt and pepper and toss to combine.

4 In a separate pan, melt the butter and fry the scallops over a high heat for 1 minute until tinged brown. Remove with a slotted spoon and add to the pasta. Tip the squid and prawns into the empty pan and fry quickly for about 2 minutes until just cooked through, then add to the pasta with the cooking juices.

5 Toss everything together over a high heat, add the tomatoes and cook for a minute. Pour the pasta mixture into a serving dish, sprinkle over the chopped parsley and serve piping hot.

TIP
When preparing the clams, discard any that remain open when tapped against a work surface.

Paella

WONDERFUL FOR ENTERTAINING and great to share, paella is best made fresh and served immediately. Paella rice is widely available in supermarkets, but risotto rice could also be used. The addition of a few cooked shell-on prawns would make this dish extra-special for entertaining. You can cook it in the oven or on the hob.

SERVES 8

4 tbsp olive oil
450g (1lb) skinless, boneless chicken thighs (about 4), thickly sliced
2 onions, chopped
1 red pepper, deseeded and diced
3 garlic cloves, crushed
500g (1lb 2oz) paella rice
1 litre (1¾ pints) hot chicken stock
a good pinch of saffron strands
175g (6oz) small, cooked peeled prawns
75g (3oz) pitted black olives in oil, drained and halved
juice of 1 small lemon
500g (1lb 2oz) fresh live mussels in their shells, cleaned (see tip)
100ml (3½fl oz) white wine
6 large tomatoes, skinned, deseeded and sliced (see tip on page 178)
salt and freshly ground black pepper
1 tbsp chopped parsley, to garnish
lemon wedges, to serve

1. Preheat the oven (if using) to 180°C/160°C fan/Gas 4.

2. Heat 2 tablespoons of the oil in a large, shallow frying pan or shallow, flameproof casserole dish. Season the chicken with salt and pepper and brown over a high heat for 2–3 minutes until golden, then remove from the pan and set aside.

3. Heat the remaining oil in the pan. Add the onions, red pepper and garlic and fry over a high heat for 4–5 minutes, then measure in the rice and mix it in well with the vegetables. Add the stock, saffron and browned chicken. Bring to the boil, then transfer to the oven, uncovered, to cook for 15–20 minutes – or cook on the hob for the same length of time – until all of the liquid has been absorbed and the rice is nearly cooked.

4. Add the prawns, olives and lemon juice and cook for a further 5 minutes, in the oven or on the hob, to heat through the prawns.

5. Meanwhile, put the mussels and wine in a large saucepan, cover with a lid and bring to the boil. Cook over a high heat for about 5 minutes, shaking the pan occasionally to ensure that they all steam evenly, until all of the mussels have opened and are cooked through. Discard any that do not open.

6. Add the mussels and strained cooking broth to the paella with the tomatoes. Check the seasoning and serve immediately, garnished with the chopped parsley, with lemon wedges on the side.

TIP
Tip the mussels into the sink or a large bowl filled with cold water to wash thoroughly. Use a small sharp knife to scrape off any barnacles and a stiff brush to clean them. Discard any with broken shells. If any mussels are open, tap them with the knife, discarding any that don't close. Pull off the beards (the strands hanging from the join between the shells) with a sharp tug, then rinse and drain in a colander.

Garlic mushroom penne gratin

AN ALL-IN-ONE DISH that can be made ahead and is perfect for serving the whole family. A mixture of field and chestnut mushrooms is given below, but you can use any mushrooms you like – closed or open cup, button, chestnut or oyster.

SERVES 6

PREPARE AHEAD
The pasta can be cooked up to 24 hours ahead, following the instructions in step 2, then kept in the fridge (see tip). The dish can be assembled fully and chilled overnight in the fridge, then cooked at 200°C/180°C fan/ Gas 6 for 30 minutes.

300g (11oz) dried penne
25g (1oz) butter
1 onion, chopped
2 garlic cloves, crushed
500g (1lb 2oz) mixed field and chestnut mushrooms, thickly sliced
200ml (7fl oz) double cream
50g (2oz) Parmesan cheese, grated
2 tbsp snipped chives
75g (3oz) mature Cheddar cheese, grated
paprika, for dusting
salt and freshly ground black pepper

1 You will need a shallow 2-litre (3½-pint) ovenproof dish.

2 Cook the pasta in boiling, salted water according to the packet instructions until just cooked. Drain and refresh in cold water to stop the pasta cooking further, then leave to drain again in the colander.

3 Melt the butter in a large frying pan. Add the onion and fry over a high heat for 4 minutes, then lower the heat, cover with a lid and cook for about 10 minutes until soft.

4 Remove the lid and turn up the heat, then add the garlic and mushrooms and fry quickly for 3–4 minutes until the mushrooms are just cooked. Season with salt and pepper.

5 Tip the drained pasta into the pan, pour in the cream and toss together. Add the Parmesan and chives, season with salt and pepper and mix until combined.

6 Pour into the ovenproof dish and sprinkle with the Cheddar cheese and paprika. Slide under a hot grill for about 5 minutes until golden and bubbling around the edges. Serve immediately with a green salad.

TIP
If making ahead, add a little more cream to the sauce as the pasta will absorb some of the moisture when standing.

SPICY TOMATO PASTA

PASTA MIXED WITH A NICELY BALANCED TOMATO SAUCE, sweet from the sugar and sharp from the vinegar – this is perfect for a quick weekday supper. It's also a great sauce to have on hand in the freezer; use for pizza toppings as well as with different types of pasta.

SERVES 6

PREPARE AHEAD
The sauce can be made up to 2 days ahead and reheated.

FREEZE
The sauce freezes well.

2 tbsp olive oil
1 large onion, finely chopped
1 celery stick, finely diced
3 garlic cloves, crushed
1 red chilli, deseeded and diced
  (see tip)
2 x 400g tins of chopped tomatoes
1 tbsp tomato purée
1 tbsp light muscovado sugar
2 tsp balsamic vinegar
300g (11oz) dried penne
salt and freshly ground black pepper

TO SERVE (OPTIONAL)
Parmesan cheese, grated
parsley sprigs

1 Heat the oil in a large frying pan, add the onion, celery, garlic and chilli and fry over a medium-high heat, stirring continuously, for about 5 minutes until softened. Add the tinned tomatoes, tomato purée, sugar and balsamic vinegar. Bring to the boil, then lower the heat, cover with a lid and simmer for 15–20 minutes until thickened and reduced. Season well with salt and pepper.

2 Once the sauce is thickened, whizz until smooth in a food processor or using a hand blender, check for seasoning and spiciness and reheat gently in a large saucepan.

3 Meanwhile, cook the pasta in boiling salted water, according to the packet instructions, until just cooked, then drain and add to the sauce. Stir to combine and serve piping hot with grated Parmesan, if you like, and a sprig of parsley.

TIP
The level of spice can be altered to taste, depending on the chilli. For a hotter sauce, keep the seeds in, increase the quantity, or use a small bird's eye chilli.

Hot & Cold Puddings

THE SELECTION OF PUDS brought together in this chapter
is designed to cater for every occasion, from warming puddings
to chilled desserts, which, while they may take a little longer
to prepare, have the advantage that they can be made well in
advance. Hot or cold, all of them are tried-and-tested
crowd pleasers.

With the busy cook in mind, I've included a number of
recipes with time-saving tricks up their sleeves. The Quickest
Ever Lemon Meringue Pie (page 238), for instance, uses a
crunchy biscuit base instead of pastry and a very straightforward
method for making the lemon filling. The Cheat's Christmas
Apricot Trifle (page 258), as the title suggests, is very quick to
prepare as I've used shop-bought custard and trifle sponges,
while the divine-tasting St Clement's Posset (page 232) can be
knocked up in minutes – just chill to serve.

The time of year may guide your choice of pudding otherwise.
In the summer, with the abundance of soft fruit available, the
Pavlova with Rosy Red Fruits and Cassis (page 253) would
be ideal, the soft meringue and whipped cream beautifully
complemented by the mixture of raspberries, blueberries and
red- and blackcurrants. The fruits are actually delicious on their

own with cream or a scoop of Easy Vanilla Ice Cream (page 226), made without recourse to an ice-cream machine and with a number of delicious variations to choose from.

When the weather gets colder, hot puddings come to the fore. For a lovely variation on the ever-popular sticky toffee pudding, you could try my Pecan and Ginger Syrup Pudding (page 240), smothered in a scrumptious butterscotch sauce that, again, could be made separately, to serve with ice cream or fresh fruit. Crumbles are a wonderful way to incorporate any fruit from the garden and I'm forever experimenting with different recipes for them. The Winter Crumble Tart (page 218) is effectively two classic puddings in one, providing the perfect vehicle for home-grown Bramleys and blackberries picked from the hedgerow.

For a real grand finale to round off a special meal, you could turn to the Celebration Chocolate Mousse Cake (page 242) or Chocolate Chip Cheesecake (page 250). Each takes a little more time to prepare but can be made well ahead, and you will be amply rewarded by the look on your guests' faces when you carry it to the table!

Winter crumble tart

The perfect combination of apple and blackberry tart with a crumble, this is ideal for using home-grown or foraged fruit in the autumn or winter. The filling is delicious, and any spare fruit can be used as an indulgent, syrupy sauce. The finished tart can be made ahead and kept for up to a day at room temperature, stored in a lidded container or covered with foil. Perfect served with a jug of hot custard.

SERVES 8

PREPARE AHEAD
The fruit can be cooked in advance and stored in a sealed container in the fridge. The whole tart can be made and cooked up to a day ahead and reheated to serve.

FREEZE
The uncooked pastry and the crumble both freeze well. Once cooked, the whole tart can be wrapped in foil and frozen. Defrost at room temperature.

FOR THE PASTRY
225g (8oz) plain flour, plus extra
    for dusting
125g (4½oz) cold butter, cut into
    cubes
30g (1oz) caster sugar
1 large egg, beaten

FOR THE FILLING
4 large Bramley apples (about
    1.2kg/2lb 10oz), peeled, cored
    and cut into small chunks
150g (5oz) caster sugar
275g (10oz) fresh blackberries

INGREDIENTS CONTINUED

1   You will need a 28cm (11in), round, loose-bottomed, fluted tart tin, 3–4cm (1¼–1½in) deep, baking paper and some baking beans. Preheat the oven to 200°C/180°C fan/Gas 6.

2   To make the pastry, measure the flour and butter into a food processor and whizz until the mixture resembles breadcrumbs (or place in a mixing bowl and rub the butter into the flour with your fingertips). Add the sugar, 1–2 tablespoons of cold water and the egg and mix again until it forms a smooth dough.

3   Tip the dough on to a lightly floured work surface and roll out into a circle large enough to line the tart tin or dish and about 3mm (⅛in) thick. Press into the base and sides of the tin and make a small lip around the top. Prick the base all over with a fork and place in the fridge to chill for 15 minutes.

4   Line the chilled pastry case with baking paper and baking beans and cook in the oven for about 15 minutes. Remove the beans and paper, then lower the oven temperature to 160°C/140°C fan/Gas 3 and bake for a further 10 minutes until crisp and golden. Set the tin aside to cool, leaving the oven on.

5   To make the filling, place the apples and sugar in a large, deep saucepan with 2 tablespoons of water over a medium heat and cook, stirring gently, for about 5 minutes. Cover with a lid and simmer, without stirring, for about 5–10 minutes until the apples begin to soften while still keeping their shape. Add the blackberries, carefully stirring them into the apples, and cook for a further 5–10 minutes until both fruits are just tender. Set aside to cool.

CONTINUED OVERLEAF

WINTER CRUMBLE TART CONTINUED

FOR THE TOPPING
175g (6oz) plain flour
100g (4oz) butter at room
    temperature, cut into cubes
50g (2oz) rolled oats
100g (4oz) demerara sugar
50g (2oz) hazelnuts, roasted and
    chopped

6 Meanwhile, make the crumble topping by measuring the flour and butter into a bowl and rubbing them together with your fingertips until the mixture resembles breadcrumbs. Add the remaining ingredients and rub in until the mixture has formed small clumps. Alternatively, whizz all the ingredients in the food processor (no need to wash this out after making the pastry).

7 Pour the cooked fruits into a colander set over a bowl to collect the juices. Spoon the fruits into the cooked pastry case. If you have any fruits left over, add them to the reserved juices. Sprinkle the crumble mixture over the top and bake in the oven (at the same temperature) for 20–25 minutes or until the crumble is golden.

8 Put the reserved juices in a saucepan and boil for 3–4 minutes until syrupy. Serve the tart warm, in slices, with the extra fruit sauce spooned over and either custard or cream.

APRICOT FRANGIPANE TART

APRICOTS AND FRANGIPANE FILLING in a crisp pastry case give a smart, delicate tart. When filling the pastry case, it's best to add the apricots at the last possible moment so that the juices don't make the base wet. If time is short, you could use a 500g pack of shop-bought short-crust pastry.

SERVES 8–10

PREPARE AHEAD
Fully made and cooked, the tart can be kept in the fridge, covered in foil, for 1 day and reheated in a low oven to serve.

FREEZE
The tart can be frozen – defrost at room temperature before serving. The pastry also freezes well, as a block or ready-rolled and lining the tart case, depending on how much space you have in your freezer.

FOR THE PASTRY
175g (6oz) plain flour, plus extra for dusting
75g (3oz) cold butter, cubed
25g (1oz) caster sugar
1 egg, beaten

FOR THE FILLING
75g (3oz) butter, softened
75g (3oz) caster sugar
2 eggs, beaten
75g (3oz) ground almonds, plus extra for sprinkling (optional – see tip overleaf)
½ tsp almond extract
2 x 400g tins of apricot halves in natural juice, drained (reserving the juice), sliced and dried (see tip overleaf)

INGREDIENTS CONTINUED

1 You will need a 28cm (11in) round, loose-bottomed fluted tart tin, 3–4cm (1¼–1½in) deep. Preheat the oven to 190°C/170°C fan/ Gas 5, and slip a heavy baking sheet inside to heat up.

2 First make the pastry, either by mixing the flour and butter in a food processor or by hand – rubbing the flour and butter together with your fingertips, until the mixture resembles breadcrumbs. Add the sugar and mix in briefly, then add the egg and ½–1 tablespoon of water. Mix until the dough just holds together.

3 Roll the pastry out on a floured surface as thinly as possible, 1–2mm (1⁄16in) thick (see tip on page 291), and use to line the tin, making a small lip around the top. Prick the base of the pastry all over with a fork.

4 Next make the frangipane filling. Place the butter and sugar in the food processor (no need to wash this out first) and whizz until creamy, blend in the eggs, then mix in the ground almonds and almond extract. Alternatively, beat together with a wooden spoon if making by hand.

5 Arrange the apricot slices over the base of the pastry and spoon the frangipane mixture on top, spreading it evenly to cover the apricots.

6 Sit the tart tin on the hot baking sheet, and bake in the oven for 45–50 minutes until the pastry is crisp and the tart is golden brown.

CONTINUED OVERLEAF

FOR THE TOPPING
about 125g (4½oz) icing sugar, sifted
1–2 tbsp apricot juice from the tin

7   To finish, make a glacé icing by mixing together the icing sugar and apricot juice, adding enough juice to give a pouring consistency and for the icing to hold its shape. Using a spoon, zigzag the icing over the tart and leave to set.

8   Remove the tart from the tin (see tip) and transfer to a serving plate. Serve warm or cold.

TIPS
Sprinkling extra ground almonds on the pastry base before adding the apricots helps to absorb extra moisture.

The apricots need to be as dry as possible to prevent the juice soaking into the pastry. Dry each one individually with kitchen paper.

An easy way of removing the tart from the tin is to stand the tart tin on one or two tins or jars; the ring around the tart can then be lowered to your work surface, leaving the tart on the base of the tin. Slide the tart off the base on to a serving plate.

EASY VANILLA ICE CREAM

SIMPLE AND DELICIOUS, and no messing around with ice-cream machines, this can be made with a food mixer or an electric hand whisk. The variations overleaf all use this easy recipe as a base for even more delicious ice-cream ideas.

MAKES 1.5 LITRES (2½ PINTS)

FREEZE
The ice cream can be kept in the freezer for up to 2 months.

4 eggs, separated (see tip on page 254)
100g (4oz) caster sugar
3 vanilla pods (see tip)
300ml (10fl oz) double pouring cream

1 Place the egg whites in the spotlessly clean bowl of a food mixer – or in a mixing bowl, if using an electric hand whisk – and whisk until they resemble a stiff white cloud. Still whisking on maximum speed, gradually add the sugar a tablespoon at a time until it is fully incorporated and the mixture is thick and glossy.

2 Use a sharp knife to slice each vanilla pod in half lengthways, then scrape out the black seeds with a teaspoon. In a separate bowl, mix the seeds in with the cream and whip until soft peaks form.

3 Add the egg yolks to the egg white mixture and stir in the cream, carefully mixing until combined. Spoon into a freezer-proof container, cover with a lid and freeze for a minimum of 8 hours or ideally overnight.

4 Remove from the freezer about 10 minutes before serving.

TIP
Don't throw away the used vanilla pods – they can be added to a jar filled with caster sugar. Leave to infuse and use the vanilla-scented sugar in any suitable baking or dessert recipes.

VARIATIONS

Different ingredients can be added to the basic vanilla ice cream before freezing, to create the following variations:

Vanilla and brownie ice cream

Crumble up 150g (5oz) chocolate brownies and stir into the vanilla ice cream.

Honeycomb ice cream

Crumble up three 80g (3oz) chocolate-covered honeycomb bars and stir into the ice cream.

Mincemeat ice cream

Stir 450g (1lb) suet-free mincemeat into the ice cream.

Chocolate ice cream

Melt 200g (7oz) dark chocolate and stir into the whisked egg whites. This works best with chocolate containing about 40 per cent cocoa solids; if you use chocolate with a higher percentage than this, be careful not to overheat it and taste before adding to the egg whites, as you may need to add a little more sugar to offset the bitterness.

For the following variations, the ice cream is made as in the main recipe but omitting the vanilla. Stir these ingredients into the ice cream mixture just before freezing.

Ginger ice cream

Add 100g (4oz) chopped preserved stem ginger and 4 tablespoons of syrup from the jar.

COFFEE AND BRANDY ICE CREAM
Add 2–3 tablespoons of coffee essence and 2 tablespoons of brandy.

RASPBERRY OR STRAWBERRY ICE CREAM
Add 150ml (5fl oz) sieved raspberry or strawberry purée.

RUM AND RAISIN ICE CREAM
Soak 100g (4oz) raisins in 4 tablespoons of rum for 2 hours, then stir into the ice cream.

MINT CHOCOLATE CHIP ICE CREAM
Add 1 teaspoon of peppermint extract and 100g (4oz) chopped dark chocolate.

LEMON OR LIME ICE CREAM
Stir in 4 tablespoons of lemon curd or the finely grated rind of 2 limes.

MANGO OR PASSION FRUIT ICE CREAM
Stir in 150ml (5fl oz) sieved mango or sieved juice from 5 passion fruit.

BLACKCURRANT OR BLACKBERRY ICE CREAM
Add about 3 tablespoons of blackcurrant cordial and 3 tablespoons of crème de cassis. Or make a sweet purée using blackcurrants or blackberries: pass the fruit through a sieve, add sugar to taste, and stir 150ml (5fl oz) into the ice cream.

St Clement's Posset

A DIVINE DESSERT and just so easy! Great for entertaining, especially as it can be made ahead of time.

MAKES 12 POTS

PREPARE AHEAD
The posset can be made 1–2 days in advance as it holds up well in the fridge.

900ml (1½ pints) double pouring cream
3 large lemons
3 oranges
200g (7oz) caster sugar
mint sprigs, to decorate

1 Measure the double cream into a small, shallow saucepan. Using a potato peeler, pare the rind from the lemons and oranges and add to the cream (see tip), stirring over a medium heat until hot but not boiling. Add the sugar to the hot cream and stir until dissolved, then remove from the heat and set aside.

2 Halve the lemons and oranges and squeeze to give 200ml (7fl oz) of juice. Add the juice to the cream and stir off the heat until thickened slightly. Strain through a sieve and discard the citrus parings.

3 Pour into 12 small pots or ramekins (see tip) and chill in the fridge for a few hours or overnight until set but still soft. Serve chilled, decorated with a sprig of mint.

TIPS
Take care to pare the orange and lemon zest thinly – you don't want too much of the white pith in with the cream or it will make it bitter.

Once the ramekins are filled, give them a light tap on the work surface to burst any air bubbles on the surface before they set. This gives a smooth, professional finish.

RASPBERRY KNICKERBOCKER GLORY

VERY SIMPLE TO PREPARE but impressive-looking when assembled, these will be loved by children and adults alike. If anyone is allergic to nuts, you could replace the pistachios with crumbled ginger biscuits. Pictured overleaf.

SERVES 6

PREPARE AHEAD
The raspberry purée can be made in advance and kept, covered, in the fridge for up to 2 days.

450g (1lb) fresh raspberries
2 tbsp icing sugar
1 ripe mango, peeled, stoned and diced
150g (5oz) fresh blueberries
12 scoops of vanilla ice cream (for homemade see page 226)
25g (1oz) pistachios, coarsely chopped

1 To make a raspberry coulis, measure 250g (9oz) of the raspberries into a food processor, add the icing sugar and whizz until smooth. Tip the raspberry purée into a sieve set over a bowl and use a metal spoon to push the fruit pulp through the sieve.

2 Divide half the diced mango between six sundae glasses. Divide half the blueberries between the glasses, placing on top of the mango. Sit one scoop of ice cream on top of each blueberry layer, drizzle over half the raspberry purée and half the whole raspberries, dividing these between the six glasses. Repeat the layering again to use the remaining ingredients and top with the chopped pistachios.

Fast gooseberry fool

If I am cooking for lots of friends or family, I will often make a fool or mousse that I can prepare well ahead and keep in the fridge. Gooseberries make a sharp, fresh-tasting creamy fool that's not too sweet. The green food colouring, while not essential, adds back the colour of the fruit which is lost during cooking. Serve with shortbread or other biscuits.

SERVES 10

PREPARE AHEAD
Cook and purée the gooseberries up to 2 days in advance, then keep chilled in the fridge and eat within 2–3 days. The completed fool can be made up to a day ahead.

1kg (2lb 3oz) fresh gooseberries (see tip), topped and tailed
250g (9oz) caster sugar
600ml (1 pint) fresh vanilla custard
600ml (1 pint) double cream, softly whipped
green food colouring (optional)
10 borage or mint flowers (optional – see tip)

1 Measure the gooseberries and sugar into a large, wide-based saucepan and add 1 tablespoon of water. Stir over a medium heat until the sugar is dissolved, then cover with a lid and cook for about 10 minutes, stirring occasionally, or until the gooseberries are tender.

2 Reserve a few cooked gooseberries for decorating. Whizz the remaining gooseberries until smooth in a food processor or using a hand blender, and pass through a sieve to give a smooth purée. Tip into a bowl and allow to cool completely.

3 Stir the custard in with the gooseberry purée, carefully fold in the whipped cream and mix until smooth. Add a dash of natural green food colouring, if you like.

4 Spoon into ten 200–300ml (7–10fl oz) glasses or pots and transfer to the fridge to set for a minimum of 6 hours. Decorate each glass or pot with a few cooked gooseberries and a borage or mint flower to serve.

TIP
If fresh gooseberries aren't available, frozen ones make a good substitute. They are a little softer when cooked, however, so don't hold their shape so well for decorating the finished pots.

If you can't get hold of borage flowers, use a sprig of mint instead to decorate each pot and add a bit of colour.

QUICKEST EVER LEMON MERINGUE PIE

THIS IS A CHEAT'S RECIPE! With no pastry and no long, complicated method for making the lemon filling, it is straightforward to prepare, and a lovely variation on the classic dish.

SERVES 6

PREPARE AHEAD
The pie can be made up to 6 hours ahead. The base and filling can be made in advance and chilled in the fridge overnight, then topped with the meringue and cooked on the day of serving.

FOR THE BASE
75g (3oz) butter
25g (1oz) demerara sugar
175g (6oz) digestive biscuits, finely crushed (see tip)

FOR THE FILLING
1 x 394g tin of full-fat, sweetened condensed milk (see tip)
3 egg yolks (see tip on page 254)
finely grated rind and juice of 2 large lemons

FOR THE TOPPING
3 egg whites (see tip on page 254)
175g (6oz) caster sugar

1 You will need a 23cm (9in) round, straight-sided or fluted ceramic tart dish, about 4cm (1½in) deep. Preheat the oven to 190°C/170°C fan/Gas 5.

2 Melt the butter in a medium saucepan, remove the pan from the heat and stir in the sugar and biscuit crumbs. Press the mixture into the flan dish using the back of a spoon to bring the crumbs up around the sides of the dish and smooth the base in an even layer.

3 To make the filling, first pour the condensed milk into a bowl, then beat in the egg yolks, lemon rind and strained juice. The mixture will appear to thicken on standing, then loosen again as soon as it is stirred. This is caused by the combination of condensed milk and lemon juice and is nothing to worry about. Pour the mixture into the biscuit-lined dish.

4 Put the egg whites into a large, spotlessly clean, grease-free bowl and, preferably with an electric hand whisk, or using a balloon whisk otherwise, whisk the egg whites until they look like clouds. Now start adding the caster sugar, a teaspoon at a time, whisking well between each addition and with the electric whisk at full speed.

5 Spoon the meringue over the surface of the filling in separate blobs, then spread gently with the back of your spoon to cover the filling to the biscuit-lined edges. Lightly swirl the surface of the meringue, then bake for 15–20 minutes or until the meringue is pale golden. Set aside for about 30 minutes to allow the filling to firm up before serving warm.

TIPS
To crush the biscuits, place in a plastic bag, seal shut and use a rolling pin to bash to a fine crumb.

Do make sure you use full-fat condensed milk, not light, or the filling will not set.

Pecan and ginger syrup pudding with butterscotch sauce

THIS IS A DIFFERENT, NUTTY TAKE on sticky toffee pudding. It's quick to make and, cooked in a traybake tin and cut into 16 slices, it will serve a large gathering. The butterscotch sauce is a real crowd pleaser. Any left over can be kept in the fridge and used to jazz up other desserts, from fresh strawberries to ice cream.

SERVES 16

PREPARE AHEAD
Make the cake 1–2 days in advance and store in an airtight tin. The sauce keeps well in the fridge for up to 3 days; it solidifies but can be reheated easily to pour.

FREEZE
The pudding can be frozen, well wrapped in greaseproof paper and foil.

250g (9oz) plain flour
1 tsp bicarbonate of soda
1 tbsp cinnamon
2 tsp ground ginger
½ tsp freshly grated nutmeg
50g (2oz) pecans, finely chopped
2 eggs, beaten
225g (8oz) light muscovado sugar
100g (4oz) golden syrup
250ml (9fl oz) milk
100g (4oz) butter, melted, plus extra
   for greasing

FOR THE SAUCE
75g (3oz) butter
75g (3oz) light muscovado sugar
3 tbsp golden syrup
300ml (10fl oz) double pouring cream
25g (1oz) pecans, finely chopped
   (see tip), plus extra to decorate

1 You will need a 30 x 23cm (12 x 9in) traybake or roasting tin. Preheat the oven to 180°C/160°C fan/Gas 4, then grease the tin with butter and line the base and sides with baking paper.

2 Measure all the dry ingredients, including the nuts but not the sugar, into a large bowl. In a separate large bowl, mix the eggs, sugar, golden syrup, milk and butter together and beat until smooth and lump-free.

3 Stir the wet ingredients into the dry ones and beat hard for about a minute until smooth. Pour into the prepared tin, spreading the batter evenly.

4 Bake in the oven for 25–30 minutes until dark in colour, springy to the touch and shrinking away from the sides of the tin.

5 To make the sauce, measure all the ingredients except the pecans into a saucepan, then stir over a gentle heat until the butter has melted and the sugar has dissolved. Bring to the boil, stirring until the sauce is bubbling, remove from the heat and mix in the pecan nuts.

6 Cut the pudding into squares and serve warm with the hot sauce poured over, and extra pecans sprinkled on top.

TIP
You can use a mini processor to chop the pecan nuts quickly.

CELEBRATION CHOCOLATE MOUSSE CAKE

THIS IS A WONDERFUL DESSERT for a celebration as it is rich and indulgent and would make a stunning centrepiece. Use chocolate with no more than 40–50 per cent cocoa solids as the richer types of chocolate can make it too bitter.

SERVES 8–10

PREPARE AHEAD
This can be made 1–2 days in advance, but without adding the fruit topping, and kept in the fridge.

FREEZE
The sponge base can be made ahead and frozen, then defrosted prior to adding the mousse layer.

FOR THE CAKE
25g (1oz) cocoa powder, plus extra for dusting
3 tbsp boiling water
100g (4oz) caster sugar
100g (4oz) self-raising flour
1 tsp baking powder
100g (4oz) baking spread, plus extra for greasing
2 large eggs
2 tbsp brandy (see tip)
225g (8oz) fresh raspberries and blueberries, to finish
pouring cream, to serve

FOR THE MOUSSE
300g (11oz) dark chocolate (no more than 40–50 per cent cocoa solids), broken into squares
450ml (15fl oz) whipping cream

1 You will need a 20cm (8in) round spring-form tin. Preheat the oven to 180°C/160°C fan/Gas 4, then grease the tin with baking spread and line the base and sides with baking paper. You need to line to the top of the tin, even though the sponge will not fill it all.

2 Measure the cocoa powder into a large bowl. Pour over the boiling water and mix with a spatula to make a paste. Add the sugar, flour, baking powder, baking spread and eggs, and beat until smooth.

3 Spoon into the prepared spring-form tin and level the top. Bake in the oven for 20–25 minutes or until springy to the touch and a skewer inserted into the middle of the cake comes out clean.

4 Brush the brandy over the top of the cake. Leave to cool in the tin.

5 To make the mousse, place the chocolate in a bowl and melt over a pan of gently simmering water, stirring until melted and smooth – take care not to let the chocolate get too hot. Set aside to cool a little.

6 Whip the cream until just forming soft peaks, fold in the melted chocolate and carefully mix until smooth and not streaky. Spoon over the cold cake, still in its tin, and level the top with a palette knife. Cover with cling film and chill in the fridge for a minimum of 4 hours, or overnight, until the mousse is firm.

7 To serve, carefully remove from the tin and set on a flat plate. Dust the top with cocoa powder and pile raspberries and blueberries into the centre of the mousse cake. Cut into slices and serve with pouring cream.

TIP
Liquid will easily soak into a warm cake, but if the cake is stone cold you may need to make some holes with a skewer before brushing the brandy over the top.

Banoffee meringue roulade

TWO OF MY FAVOURITE DESSERTS combined in one – banoffee pie and meringue roulade. The meringue has a lovely marshmallowy texture that goes beautifully with the creamy banoffee filling. Also pictured overleaf.

SERVES 8

PREPARE AHEAD
Make on the day and chill for a couple of hours, wrapped in its greaseproof paper, before serving.

FREEZE
Wrap in foil to freeze. Defrost thoroughly in the fridge and drizzle with the toffee sauce before serving. While the meringue freezes very well, the bananas do discolour a little.

5 egg whites
275g (10oz) caster sugar

FOR THE FILLING
25g (1oz) butter, plus extra for greasing
25g (1oz) light muscovado sugar
400ml (14fl oz) double cream
1 large banana, thinly sliced

1. You will need a 33 x 23cm (13 x 9in) Swiss roll tin. Preheat the oven to 200°C/180°C fan/Gas 6. Grease the tin with butter and line with baking paper.

2. Place the egg whites in a large, spotlessly clean, grease-free bowl and, using an electric hand whisk or food mixer, whisk on full speed until very stiff. Gradually add the sugar, a teaspoon at a time and still on full speed, whisking well between each addition. Continue to whisk until very stiff and glossy and all the sugar has been incorporated.

3. Tip the meringue mixture into the prepared tin, spreading it out evenly, then slide into the oven and bake for about 8 minutes until very golden. Lower the temperature to 160°C/140°C fan/Gas 3 and bake the meringue for a further 15 minutes until firm to the touch.

4. While the meringue is cooking, make the banoffee filling. Heat the butter, sugar and 150ml (5fl oz) of the cream in a saucepan over a medium heat, stirring until the butter has melted and the sugar dissolved. Bring to the boil, stirring until the mixture begins to bubble. Allow to boil for a couple of minutes, then remove from the heat to cool down completely.

5. When the meringue has finished cooking, take it out of the oven and turn upside down on to a sheet of non-stick baking paper, removing the tin. Carefully peel the paper from the base of the cooked meringue and allow to cool.

6. Whip the remaining cream until it forms soft peaks, stir in the sliced banana and gently fold in half the toffee sauce to give a swirled effect. Spread evenly over the meringue. Using the baking paper to help you, roll up the meringue fairly tightly from one of the long ends, to form a roulade. Drizzle over the remaining toffee sauce and chill well before serving.

7. Transfer to a serving plate, remove the paper and cut into slices to serve.

MINI APPLE AND ALMOND CAKES

ONE OF MY FAVOURITE BAKES is a recipe for apple cake I created many years ago. This is a version of the same recipe but made up into individual cakes, which could be served warm as a dinner party dessert or cold as a delicious picnic treat. It is important to weigh all the ingredients accurately or a dip may appear in the top of the cakes due to the moisture in the apple.

MAKES 6 CAKES

PREPARE AHEAD
These can be made in advance and stored in an airtight tin for 3 days.

FREEZE
The cooked cakes freeze well.

75g (3oz) butter, melted, plus extra for greasing
100g (4oz) caster sugar
100g (4oz) self-raising flour, plus extra for dusting
1 egg, beaten
½ tsp almond extract
60g (2½oz) Bramley apples, peeled and thinly sliced
15g (½oz) flaked almonds

1   You will need six 7cm (2¾in) cooking rings (or see tip). Preheat the oven to 180°C/160°C fan/Gas 4. Grease the inside of the cooking rings with a little butter and dust with flour, then arrange the cooking rings on a baking sheet lined with baking paper.

2   Pour the melted butter into a large bowl, add the sugar, flour, egg and almond extract and mix together until combined. Spoon a little of the mixture into the base of each ring, arrange some of the apple slices over the batter and spoon the remaining cake mixture on top, levelling with the back of a teaspoon.

3   Scatter each cake with flaked almonds and bake in the oven for 25–30 minutes or until well risen and golden brown. Set aside to cool for about 10 minutes before removing the rings. Serve warm with a dollop of crème fraîche.

TIP
If you don't have cooking rings, or fewer than the six needed here, you can make your own using small (200g) baked bean tins. Remove the top and bottom of each tin and grease with butter and dust with flour as in the recipe – taking care with the sharp edges – before filling with the cake mixture. Alternatively, you could use any straight-sided bun tins with a loose bottom.

CHOCOLATE CHIP CHEESECAKE

THIS RICH AND INDULGENT CHEESECAKE has a truffle-like texture and an unusual, buttery shortbread base. It's ideal for entertaining as the basic cheesecake and chocolate decorations can be made in advance and stored in the fridge before assembling with the whipped cream and grated chocolate when you're ready to serve.

....

SERVES 10–12

PREPARE AHEAD
The cheesecake can be made up to 2 days ahead and stored, covered, in the fridge before decorating on the day.

FREEZE
This can be frozen on the tin base or removed from the tin, well wrapped, without the decoration.

FOR THE BASE
25g (1oz) butter, plus extra for greasing
150g (5oz) shortbread biscuits, finely crushed (see tip on page 238)

FOR THE TOPPING
300g (11oz) dark chocolate (no more than 40 per cent cocoa solids – see tip overleaf)
2 eggs, beaten
400g (14oz) full-fat cream cheese
150ml (5fl oz) full-fat soured cream
50g (2oz) dark chocolate chips or drops

INGREDIENTS CONTINUED

1 You will need a 20cm (8in) round, deep spring-form cake tin and a piping bag for decorating the cheesecake. Preheat the oven to 160°C/140°C fan/Gas 3, then grease the base of the tin with butter and line with baking paper.

2 Melt the butter in a small saucepan over a low heat. Stir in the crushed biscuits, then tip into the prepared cake tin and press evenly over the base of the tin. Place in the fridge to chill while you make the cheesecake topping.

3 Break the chocolate into a bowl and melt over a pan of hot water (do not allow the chocolate to become too hot), stirring occasionally with a spoon, until runny and smooth.

4 Put the eggs, cream cheese and soured cream into a separate bowl and whisk until just smooth. Pour in the melted chocolate and whisk for a minute until smooth, then stir in the chocolate chips or drops.

5 Spoon into the tin and spread evenly over the chilled biscuit base. Bake in the oven for 45–50 minutes until firm around the edges and with a slight wobble in the middle.

6 Remove from the oven. Carefully run a small palette knife around the inside edge of the tin to release the cooked cheesecake, then allow to cool in the tin before transferring to the fridge to chill. Once chilled, remove the outside ring of the tin and lift the base on to a serving plate, removing the paper lining.

CONTINUED OVERLEAF

CHOCOLATE CHIP CHEESECAKE continued

To serve
100g (4oz) dark chocolate (no more than 40–50 per cent cocoa solids)
300ml (10fl oz) whipping cream, softly whipped

7   Finely grate a third of the chocolate for serving. Melt the remaining chocolate over a pan of simmering water and, once melted, pipe on to baking paper in flower shapes or a design of your choice. Transfer to the fridge to set.

8   Spread the whipped cream in a thin layer on top of the cake and sprinkle over the grated chocolate, then pipe or spoon the remaining cream around the edge of the cake and add the chocolate decorations. Serve chilled, cut into wedges.

TIP
I used a dark chocolate with a lower percentage of cocoa solids as it tastes less bitter and therefore means that no sugar needs to be included in the cheesecake topping.

PAVLOVA WITH ROSY RED FRUITS AND CASSIS

PAVLOVA IS A GREAT FAMILY FAVOURITE. The meringue base needs to be made ahead but can be quickly filled on the day – ideally shortly before serving. It is lovely to serve with extra fruit salad on the side. If you don't have time to make the pavlova, simply serve the red fruits on their own, warm or cold, with cream. Pictured overleaf and on pages 256–7.

SERVES 6–8

PREPARE AHEAD
The pavlova can be stored in an airtight container for up to 2 weeks before adding the topping. It can be filled in advance and kept in the fridge for a day. The red fruit salad can be kept in the fridge for 3–4 days.

FOR THE MERINGUE
3 egg whites (see tip overleaf)
175g (6oz) caster sugar
1 tsp white wine vinegar
1 level tsp cornflour
300ml (10fl oz) double cream, whipped

FOR THE FRUIT SALAD
225g (8oz) redcurrants, stalks removed (see tip overleaf)
225g (8oz) blackcurrants, stalks removed (see tip overleaf)
225g (8oz) blackberries
175g (6oz) caster sugar
175g (6oz) blueberries
450g (1lb) raspberries
2–3 tbsp crème de cassis

1 Preheat the oven to 160°C/140°C fan/Gas 3. Lay a piece of baking paper on a baking sheet and draw a 20cm (8in) circle on it using the bottom of a round cake tin as a template.

2 Put the egg whites in a large, spotlessly clean, grease-free bowl and whisk until stiff on the highest setting with an electric hand whisk or in a free-standing food mixer. Still whisking on maximum speed, gradually add generous teaspoonfuls of the sugar until the mixture is stiff and shiny and standing in peaks.

3 Blend the vinegar and cornflour together in a cup and mix until smooth. Stir into the meringue mixture.

4 Spoon the mixture on to the lined baking sheet, spreading it out to fill the circle and building up the sides of the pavlova so they are higher than the centre to create a large nest.

5 Slide into the middle of the oven, turn the heat down to 150°C/130°C fan/Gas 2 and bake for about an hour, or until the cooked meringue comes away easily from the paper. The pavlova will be a pale, creamy colour rather than white. Turn off the oven and leave the pavlova inside to become cold for several hours or ideally overnight.

6 Meanwhile, make the fruit salad. Put the redcurrants, blackcurrants and blackberries in a large saucepan with the sugar and warm gently over a very low heat, stirring occasionally, for 10–15 minutes. The sugar will dissolve in the juices from the fruits, so no additional water is needed. When the fruits are warm and the sugar has dissolved, add the blueberries.

7 Pour the fruits into a serving dish and allow to cool before putting in the fridge to chill. (If serving the fruit salad warm on its own, add the

CONTINUED OVERLEAF

PAVLOVA WITH ROSY RED FRUITS AND CASSIS

CONTINUED

raspberries and crème de cassis at this stage, stirring in gently to keep the fruits whole.)

8 Once the pavlova is cold, spoon the whipped cream into the centre. Gently stir the raspberries and crème de cassis into the fruit salad and pour the fruits into a sieve set over a bowl. Spoon half the drained fruits on top of the cream-filled pavlova and serve the remaining fruit salad and liquid in a bowl on the side.

TIPS

It's best to separate the eggs one at a time to minimise the possibility of contaminating the whole lot with egg yolk, as this will prevent the egg whites from whisking properly.

Use a fork to strip the currants from their stalks.

To fix the baking paper on to the baking tray, put four blobs of meringue under each corner of the baking paper.

Cheat's christmas apricot trifle

No Christmas table is complete without a trifle – this one's a cheat because I use shop-bought custard and sponges. If making this for adults only, you could add an extra 1–2 tablespoons of brandy to soak the cake. The trifle benefits from being made in advance as the flavours have a chance to mingle and develop.

SERVES 8

PREPARE AHEAD
This can be made a day ahead and kept, covered, in the fridge. Scatter over the nuts just before serving so they stay crisp.

10–12 trifle sponges, weighing 225g (8oz) in total
about 4 tbsp apricot jam
2 x 410g tins of apricot halves in light syrup
1½ tbsp brandy
1 x 500g carton of fresh vanilla custard
150ml (5fl oz) whipping cream, whipped to soft peaks
30g (1oz) flaked almonds, toasted

1 You will need a 2.5-litre (4½-pint) glass trifle dish with a wide base.

2 Slice each trifle sponge in half horizontally. Spread the apricot jam over one half of each slice and sandwich together with the other half.

3 Drain the tinned apricots, reserving 3 tablespoons of syrup from the tin, and chop the apricot halves into chunks.

4 Arrange half the sandwiched-together trifle sponges in the base of a glass trifle bowl and press them in. Pour over half the apricot syrup and half the brandy until all the sponge is soaked. Scatter half the chopped apricots over the top.

5 Repeat with another, final, layer of sponge, apricot syrup, brandy and apricots. Spoon over the custard, spread or pipe over the cream and scatter with the toasted flaked almonds.

TIPS
If you don't have a large trifle bowl, this could be made easily in 12 individual wine glasses, or other pretty glasses. Perfect for a Christmas fork buffet.

Depending on the width of your trifle dish, the number of trifle sponges you need may vary slightly.

Tea Time

WHEN IT COMES TO TEA TIME, the old saying 'a little of what you fancy does you good' couldn't be more appropriate, in my view. There really is nothing more cheering than a slice of freshly made cake or some other home-baked treat served not just for afternoon tea but at any time of day.

No book about favourites would be complete without my Lemon Drizzle Cake, of course. The version that I've provided here (pages 276–9) is actually four lemon drizzles in one – two different sizes of traybake, a loaf and a round cake – as people constantly ask me for different ways of presenting the basic recipe. The traybakes and loaves would be ideal for serving a crowd – at a summer fete or a picnic, perhaps – while you might prefer to make the round version for sharing with friends at home.

Granny's Little Shortbread Biscuits (page 264), three delicious flavours made from one batch of dough, is another highly versatile recipe, perfect for preparing at home with children –

each child could make a different type of biscuit. You could package them for fetes or fund-raising events, pop them into a lunchbox or just have a tin of them to hand for the family to help themselves. The Pecan and Cinnamon Ripple Squares (page 286) would make a lovely lunchbox treat as well, while the Mincemeat and Orange Feathered Tarts (page 291), topped with grated marzipan instead of pastry, offer something a bit different for the festive season.

Updating classic recipes is something that I really enjoy and there are some great variations on older themes to choose from here. The Tiramisu Cake (page 282), for instance, transforms the traditional Italian dessert into a wonderfully light and not too sweet sponge, while the Sweet Nutty Twists (page 288) are like a sweet version of cheese straws – divine with a cup of coffee or for serving at the end of a meal with a chilled mousse or fool.

GRANNY'S LITTLE SHORTBREAD BISCUITS

THESE ARE MY FAVOURITE BISCUITS to make with my grandchildren – three classic biscuit flavours from just one batch of dough. The different types can be made and cut out at the same time, if you prefer, but each sheet of biscuits should be baked separately to ensure even cooking. Once one batch is baked, transfer them to a wire rack to cool while you cook the next.

MAKES 20 OF EACH VARIETY

PREPARE AHEAD
These biscuits can be stored in an airtight container for 3–4 days. The dough can be stored in the fridge for 1–2 days before flavouring and shaping.

FOR THE BISCUIT DOUGH
175g (6oz) butter, softened
75g (3oz) caster sugar
175g (6oz) plain flour, plus extra for dusting
75g (3oz) semolina

FOR THE CHOCOLATE CHIP BISCUITS
50g (2oz) milk or plain chocolate chips

FOR THE LEMON BISCUITS
finely grated zest of 1 lemon
1–2 tbsp demerara sugar

FOR THE ALMOND BISCUITS
1 tsp almond extract
40g (1½oz) flaked almonds

1 Preheat the oven to 180°C/160°C fan/Gas 4 and line three baking sheets with baking paper.

2 To make the biscuit dough, measure the butter, sugar, flour and semolina into the bowl of an electric food mixer and mix until a soft dough is formed, taking care not to over-beat. Alternatively, add the butter and sugar to a mixing bowl and beat with a wooden spoon until soft and creamy, then stir in the flour and semolina. Divide the dough evenly into three and dust your work surface with flour before kneading each batch.

3 To make the CHOCOLATE CHIP BISCUITS, knead the chocolate chips into one portion of dough, shape into 20 balls and arrange, spaced well apart, on one of the baking sheets. Press down with the back of a fork to make discs about 5cm (2in) in diameter and bake in the oven for 10–12 minutes or until golden brown.

4 To make the LEMON BISCUITS, knead the lemon zest into the second portion of dough. Roll into a long sausage shape (about 20cm/8in long) and roll in the demerara sugar. Wrap in cling film and leave in the freezer for about 30 minutes until firm and nearly frozen. (See also tip.) Slice into 20 even rounds, each about 1cm (½in) thick, arrange on a baking sheet, spaced well apart, and bake for about 10 minutes or until pale golden brown.

5 To make the ALMOND BISCUITS, knead the almond extract into the remaining portion of dough, along with most of the flaked almonds. Shape into 20 small balls and arrange on the third baking sheet, spaced apart. Place a few almonds on top of each ball of dough and press flat with the back of a fork into discs about 5cm (2in) in diameter. Bake for about 10 minutes or until golden brown.

TIP
By freezing the roll of lemon biscuit dough first, you can create perfect round discs for the biscuits, whereas the others are a little more rustically rough around the edges!

LUCY'S STRAWBERRY SLICES

LUCY HAS WORKED WITH ME FOR 25 YEARS! A twist on the classic Victoria sandwich, her slices look adorable and are, of course, divine to eat! Also pictured overleaf.

Also pictured overleaf.

MAKES 27 SLICES

PREPARE AHEAD
The cake on its own, without the filling, will keep well in an airtight tin for a day. Once filled, the cakes can be stored in the fridge up to 8 hours ahead.

FREEZE
Wrap the cake, without the filling, in cling film and foil and store in the freezer.

225g (8oz) butter, softened, or baking spread, plus extra for greasing
4 eggs
225g (8oz) caster sugar
300g (11oz) self-raising flour
2 level tsp baking powder
4 tbsp milk
1 tsp vanilla extract

FOR THE FILLING
2 tbsp strawberry jam
1 tsp lemon juice
300g (11oz) small fresh strawberries, hulled and cut in half
300ml (10fl oz) double cream, whipped
200ml (7fl oz) full-fat crème fraîche
icing sugar, for dusting

1 You will need a 30 x 23cm (12 x 9in) traybake tin. Preheat the oven to 180°C/160°C fan/Gas 4, then grease the tin with butter or baking spread and line the base and sides with greased baking paper.

2 Measure all the cake ingredients into a large bowl and beat well for about 2 minutes until well blended. Turn the mixture into the prepared tin and level the top.

3 Bake in the oven for 35 minutes or until the cake has shrunk from the sides of the tin and springs back when pressed in the centre with your fingertips. Leave to cool in the tin.

4 Remove the cake from the tin and trim the edges so that they are perfectly straight. Cut the cake lengthways into three strips, then cut across each strip to give nine 7 x 3cm (2¾ x 1½in) oblong slices. Cut each slice in half horizontally ready for filling as you would a sandwich.

5 Spoon the jam into a bowl with the lemon juice and blend together, then toss the strawberries in the jam to give a glaze. Mix the whipped cream and crème fraîche together and spread or pipe a fairly thick layer over the base of each half-sponge. Arrange two or three glazed pieces of strawberry on top and sit the top half of the sponge on top. Dust with icing sugar to serve.

GINGER AND SULTANA ICED BUNS

THESE WONDERFULLY MOIST BUNS are covered with glacé icing and use preserved stem ginger chopped up for topping the little cakes, with the ginger syrup added to the sponge.

MAKES 12 BUNS

PREPARE AHEAD
These can be made 2–3 days in advance and kept in an airtight tin.

FREEZE
The buns will freeze well without the icing and chopped ginger added on top.

150g (5oz) butter, softened
3 eggs
100g (4oz) golden caster sugar
150g (5oz) self-raising flour
1 tsp ground ginger
2 tbsp ginger syrup from the jar
100g (4oz) sultanas

FOR THE TOPPING
150g (5oz) icing sugar
2 tbsp ginger syrup from the jar
1½ tbsp warm water
2 small bulbs of stem ginger,
   chopped into small pieces

1 You will need a 12-hole bun tin. Preheat the oven to 180°C/160°C fan/Gas 4 and line the tin with paper cases.

2 Measure the butter, eggs, sugar, flour, ground ginger and syrup into a large bowl and beat until smooth. Stir in the sultanas.

3 Spoon evenly between the paper cases and bake in the oven for about 20 minutes until golden and springy to the touch. Remove from the tin and place on a wire rack to cool before adding the icing.

4 To make the icing, sift the icing sugar into a bowl, stir in the ginger syrup and gradually mix in the water to give a glossy icing. Spoon over the cold buns and sprinkle with the chopped stem ginger.

MINI BAKEWELL TARTS

THE CLASSIC cherry Bakewell recipe – classic size, classically delicious!

MAKES 12 TARTS

PREPARE AHEAD
These can be prepared up to 2 days ahead and kept in an airtight tin.

FREEZE
These freeze well without the glacé icing. Once baked, cool completely and pack in a sturdy box, so they don't get damaged in the freezer. They can be iced and finished with the cherries once defrosted.

FOR THE PASTRY
150g (5oz) plain flour, plus extra for dusting
75g (3oz) butter, cubed, plus extra for greasing
35g (1¼oz) icing sugar
1 small egg, beaten

FOR THE FILLING
100g (4oz) butter, softened
100g (4oz) caster sugar
3 eggs
100g (4oz) ground almonds
½ tsp almond extract
60g (2½oz) raspberry jam

FOR THE TOPPING
100g (4oz) icing sugar
about 3tsp water
6 glacé cherries, halved, to decorate

1 You will need a 12-hole bun tin and an 8cm (3in) pastry cutter (see tip). Grease the moulds of the bun tin with butter.

2 To make the pastry, measure the flour and butter into a food processor and whizz until the mixture resembles breadcrumbs. Alternatively, put the flour and butter in a bowl and rub in with your fingertips. Add the icing sugar and egg and mix again to form a dough.

3 Roll out the dough on a floured work surface until about 3mm (⅛in) thick. Use the pastry cutter to stamp out 12 discs and then line each mould of the bun tin with these. Cover the tin with cling film and chill in the fridge for 30 minutes.

4 Preheat the oven to 200°C/180°C fan/Gas 6 and place a baking sheet inside to get very hot.

5 To make the filling, add the butter and sugar to the food processor or bowl (no need to wash it out first) and whizz until creamy. Add the eggs, ground almonds and almond extract, then whizz again to combine. (At this stage, the mixture will look a little curdled.)

6 Remove the bun tin from the fridge and prick the base of each pastry case with a fork. Spoon a little of the jam into the centre of each pastry case, then add the almond mixture, dividing it evenly between the cases.

7 Set the bun tin on the hot baking sheet in the oven and bake for 15–18 minutes or until the pastry is cooked and the tarts are golden on top. Remove from the tin and place on a wire rack to cool, before adding the icing.

8 Sift the icing sugar into a bowl and mix with as much water as needed (about 3 teaspoons) to make a smooth glacé icing, adding a teaspoonful at a time. Spoon the icing on top of the cold tarts and top with half a cherry in the middle of each one. Leave to set.

TIP
If you don't have an 8cm (3in) pastry cutter, go for a slightly larger rather than a smaller one. There is plenty of filling in this recipe, and tarts with slightly deeper sides would hold the filling well.

Malted chocolate cake

THIS CAKE IS THE PERFECT FAMILY TREAT, and a real crowd-pleaser. The malt extract gives a lovely creaminess to the sponge, while the malted chocolate flavour is echoed in the cake's topping.

SERVES 8–10

PREPARE AHEAD
The filling will remain soft and ready to use in a bowl covered with cling film for 2–3 days. The finished cake can be kept in an airtight container for up to a day.

FREEZE
Freeze the cake and icing separately, then defrost at room temperature and assemble when ready to serve.

30g (1oz) malted chocolate
   drink powder
30g (1oz) cocoa powder
225g (8oz) butter, softened, plus
   extra for greasing
225g (8oz) caster sugar
225g (8oz) self-raising flour
1 tsp baking powder
4 eggs

FOR THE ICING
3 tbsp malted chocolate drink
   powder
1½ tbsp hot milk
125g (4½oz) butter, softened
250g (9oz) icing sugar, plus extra
   for dusting
50g (2oz) dark chocolate (at least
   50 per cent cocoa solids), melted
1 tbsp boiling water
about 20 Maltesers, to decorate

1 You will need two 20cm (8in) round sandwich tins. Preheat the oven to 180°C/160°C fan/Gas 4 and grease the tins with butter and line the bases with baking paper.

2 Measure the malted chocolate drink powder and cocoa powder into a large bowl, pour over 2 tablespoons of water and mix to a paste. Add the remaining cake ingredients and beat until smooth.

3 Divide evenly between the prepared tins and bake in the oven for 20–25 minutes. Set aside in the tins to cool for 5 minutes, then turn out on to a wire rack to cool completely.

4 To make the icing, measure the malted chocolate drink powder into a bowl, add the hot milk and mix until smooth. Add the butter, icing sugar and melted chocolate and mix again until smooth, then add the boiling water to give a gloss to the icing.

5 Place one cake on a plate and spread over half the icing. Sandwich with the other cake and spread (or pipe) the remaining icing on top, using the tip of a rounded palette knife to create a swirled effect from the centre to the edge of the cake. Arrange the Maltesers over the top and dust with icing sugar before serving.

LEMON DRIZZLE CAKES

I HAVE BEEN MAKING LEMON DRIZZLE CAKE for as long as I can remember – since the 1960s at least! This is the recipe I am most asked for when stopped in the street. It is important to spoon the glaze on to the cake while it's still warm so the lemon juice soaks in properly. If you do not have granulated sugar for the glaze, you can use caster sugar, although it will not give quite such a crunchy result. Lemon balm works well as an alternative for lemon verbena if you can't get hold of any, or you could use finely chopped lemon thyme leaves to give a slightly more distinctive herby flavour. Lemon verbena, or one of the substitute herbs, adds a lovely depth of flavour but it could be omitted if necessary.

LEMON DRIZZLE TRAYBAKE

MAKES ABOUT 16 PIECES

PREPARE AHEAD
Any of these cakes can be stored in an airtight container for 3–4 days.

FREEZE
These cakes can all be frozen for up to 1 month.

225g (8oz) baking spread, straight from the fridge, or softened butter, plus extra for greasing
225g (8oz) caster sugar
275g (10oz) self-raising flour
2 level tsp baking powder
4 eggs
4 tbsp milk
grated rind of 2 lemons
1 heaped tbsp very finely chopped lemon verbena

FOR THE GLAZE
175g (6oz) granulated sugar
juice of 2 lemons

1 You will need a 30 x 23cm (12 x 9in) traybake or roasting tin. Preheat the oven to 180°C/160°C fan/Gas 4. Grease the tin with baking spread or butter and line the base with baking paper.

2 Measure all the cake ingredients into a large bowl and beat for about 2 minutes until well blended. Turn the mixture into the prepared tin and level the top.

3 Bake in the oven for 35–40 minutes until the cake has shrunk a little from the sides of the tin and springs back when lightly touched with a fingertip in the centre of the cake. Leave to cool for 5 minutes in the tin, then lift out, with the lining paper still attached, and place on a wire rack set over a tray.

4 While the cake is baking, make the topping. Mix the granulated sugar with the lemon juice and stir to a runny consistency. Brush or spoon the sugar and lemon all over the surface of the warm cake and leave to set. Remove the lining paper and cut into slices to serve.

LARGE LEMON DRIZZLE TRAYBAKE

MAKES 24 SQUARES

350g (12oz) baking spread, straight from the fridge, or softened butter, plus extra for greasing
350g (12oz) caster sugar
425g (15oz) self-raising flour
1½ level tsp baking powder
6 eggs
6 tbsp milk
grated rind of 3 lemons
3 tbsp very finely chopped lemon verbena

FOR THE GLAZE
250g (9oz) granulated sugar
juice of 3 lemons

1　You will need a 39 x 25cm (15 x 10in) large traybake or roasting tin. Preheat the oven to 180°C/160°C fan/Gas 4. Grease the tin with baking spread or butter and line the base with baking paper.

2　Follow steps 2–4 of the Lemon Drizzle Traybake on the previous page for preparing, baking and icing the cake, baking in the oven for 35–40 minutes.

TIP
As this is such a large traybake, you may find you need to use 2 sheets of baking paper.

LEMON DRIZZLE LOAVES

EACH LOAF SERVES 8

225g (8oz) baking spread, straight from the fridge, or softened butter, plus extra for greasing
225g (8oz) caster sugar
275g (10oz) self-raising flour
1 level tsp baking powder
4 eggs
4 tbsp milk
grated rind of 1 lemon
1 heaped tbsp very finely chopped lemon verbena

FOR THE GLAZE
75g (3oz) granulated sugar
about 1 tbsp lemon juice

1　You will need two 450g (1lb) loaf tins. Preheat the oven to 180°C/160°C fan/Gas 4. Grease the tins with baking spread or butter and line the base and sides with greased baking paper.

2　Follow steps 2–4 of the Lemon Drizzle Traybake on the previous page for preparing, baking and icing the loaves, baking in the oven for about 35 minutes.

ROUND LEMON DRIZZLE CAKE

SERVES 8–10

225g (8oz) baking spread, straight
   from the fridge, or softened butter,
   plus extra for greasing
225g (8oz) caster sugar
275g (10oz) self-raising flour
1 level tsp baking powder
4 eggs
4 tbsp milk
grated rind of 2 lemons
2 tbsp very finely chopped lemon
   verbena

FOR THE GLAZE
175g (6oz) granulated sugar
juice of 2 lemons

1 You will need a 20cm (8in) round, deep cake tin. Preheat the oven to 180°C/160°C fan/Gas 4. Grease the tin with baking spread or butter and line the base and sides with baking paper.

2 Follow steps 2–4 of the Lemon Drizzle Traybake on page 276 for preparing, baking and icing the loaves, baking in the oven for about 1 hour to 1 hour 10 minutes. If the cake starts getting too brown during cooking, cover with foil after 45 minutes.

Tiramisu cake

A LIGHT, FATLESS SPONGE with a mascarpone icing, this would be lovely to serve as a dessert for a special celebration or for a teatime treat. As it's not overly sweet, it's also ideal for anyone who doesn't have a particularly sweet tooth.

SERVES 8–10

PREPARE AHEAD
The cake can be made and fully assembled a day ahead. Keep in the fridge until ready to serve.

FREEZE
The sponge cakes can be frozen without the mascarpone filling.

butter, for greasing
4 large eggs
100g (4oz) caster sugar
100g (4oz) self-raising flour
1 tbsp instant coffee granules
1 tbsp boiling water

FOR THE SOAKING LIQUID
50ml (2fl oz) brandy
3 tbsp freshly prepared coffee
3 tbsp boiling water

FOR THE ICING
2 x 250g tubs of full-fat mascarpone cheese
150ml (5fl oz) double cream
3 tbsp icing sugar, sifted
4 tbsp grated plain chocolate (at least 50 per cent cocoa solids)

1 You will need two 20cm (8in) round sandwich tins. Preheat the oven to 180°C/160°C fan/Gas 4. Grease the tins with butter and line the bases with baking paper.

2 Combine all the ingredients for the soaking liquid in a bowl and set aside.

3 Place the eggs and sugar in a large bowl and whisk together until the mixture is very pale and thick and the beaters leave a light trail on the surface when lifted. As this will take about 5 minutes, it's best to do this using a free-standing food mixer, if you have one, otherwise use an electric hand whisk. Sift over the flour and fold in gently using a metal spoon or spatula, taking care not to over-mix. Dissolve the coffee in the hot water and stir into the cake mix.

4 Divide the mixture evenly between the prepared sandwich tins, tilting each tin to level the surface. Bake in the oven for 20–25 minutes or until risen, golden and springy to the touch. Turn the cakes out on to a wire rack and remove the baking paper. Brush the soaking liquid over each cake and leave to cool completely.

5 Meanwhile, place the mascarpone cheese in a large bowl and beat until smooth using a wooden spoon or an electric hand whisk on a low setting. Gradually beat in the double cream and icing sugar to make a creamy, spreadable icing.

6 Place one sponge, soaked side up, on a flat serving plate. Spoon over half of the mascarpone icing and scatter over half the grated chocolate. Place the second sponge on top, soaked side down, spread over the remaining icing and dust with the remaining chocolate.

LIME AND POLENTA CAKE

THIS IS PERFECT TO SERVE WITH COFFEE or as a dessert, warm with a dollop of crème fraîche. Buttery and very moist, it has the advantage of being naturally gluten-free, with an interesting grainy texture from the ground almonds and polenta.

SERVES 8

PREPARE AHEAD
The cake can be made in advance and stored in an airtight container for 2–3 days.

FREEZE
Wrap and freeze the cooled cake, then defrost at room temperature.

300g (11oz) butter, softened, plus extra for greasing
300g (11oz) caster sugar
finely grated rind and juice of 2 limes
4 eggs, beaten
300g (11oz) ground almonds
150g (5oz) polenta
1 tsp baking powder

FOR THE GLAZE
finely grated rind and juice of 1 lime
75g (3oz) caster sugar
icing sugar, for dusting

1 You will need a 23cm (9in) round spring-form tin. Preheat the oven to 160°C/140°C fan/Gas 3. Grease the tin with butter and line the base with baking paper.

2 Put the butter, sugar and lime rind into a large bowl and beat with an electric hand whisk until pale and fluffy. Gradually whisk in the eggs, then add the ground almonds, polenta, lime juice and baking powder and carefully fold in until thoroughly combined.

3 Spoon into the prepared tin and level the surface. Bake in the oven for about 1 hour 15 minutes or until a skewer inserted into the middle of the cake comes out clean and the sponge is golden brown and springy to the touch. If the top of the cake is getting too brown before then, cover with foil. Set aside while you make the glaze.

4 Heat the lime rind and juice, sugar and 2 tablespoons of water in a small pan, stirring over a low heat until the sugar has dissolved, then simmering for 2–3 minutes until syrupy. Prick the surface of the cake with the skewer, spoon the hot syrup evenly over the warm sponge and leave to cool completely in the tin.

5 Remove from the tin, transfer to a serving plate and dust with icing sugar. Serve warm or cold, sliced into wedges, with a dollop of crème fraîche.

PECAN AND CINNAMON RIPPLE SQUARES

A WONDERFULLY BUTTERY CAKE with a sugary swirl and a delicious crunch from the pecans, this is like a sponge version of a pecan Danish.

MAKES 16 SQUARES

PREPARE AHEAD
The cake can be made 1–2 days ahead and kept in an airtight container.

FREEZE
Wrap the cake to freeze, defrosting at room temperature.

225g (8oz) butter, softened, plus extra for greasing
4 large eggs
225g (8oz) self-raising flour
225g (8oz) caster sugar
2 tsp baking powder
1 tsp vanilla extract

FOR THE RIPPLE
100g (4oz) pecan nuts
25g (1oz) light muscovado sugar
1 heaped tsp ground cinnamon

1 You will need a 30 x 23cm (12 x 9in) traybake tin. Preheat the oven to 180°C/160°C fan/Gas 4. Grease the tin with butter and line the base and sides with baking paper.

2 First make the pecan ripple mixture. Place 75g (3oz) of the pecan nuts in a food processor and whizz until finely ground. Mix in a bowl with the muscovado sugar and cinnamon, then set aside. Chop the remaining pecans by hand and set them aside for the topping.

3 Measure the ingredients for the sponge into a bowl and beat until combined and smooth.

4 Spread just under half of the sponge mixture over the base of the prepared tin. Spoon over two-thirds of the pecan ripple mix in an even layer. Spoon over the rest of the cake batter and gently level the surface with a small palette knife. Drag the handle of a teaspoon in a swirly pattern through the layered batter. Sprinkle over the rest of the pecan ripple and scatter over the reserved chopped pecans.

5 Bake in the oven for 25–30 minutes or until risen, golden and just firm to the touch. Remove from the oven and cool in the tin for 5–10 minutes, then turn out on to a wire rack to cool down completely. Cut into squares to serve.

SWEET NUTTY TWISTS

A SWEET VERSION OF CHEESE STRAWS but half the size, these little biscuits are perfect to serve with coffee after dinner, for a snack or to accompany a cold dessert.

MAKES 30 STRAWS

50g (2oz) shelled pistachio nuts, finely chopped
50g (2oz) chopped almonds
25g (1oz) caster sugar
1½ tsp almond extract
1 x 320g pack of ready-rolled, all-butter puff pastry
plain flour, for dusting
1 egg white, beaten with a fork until lightly frothy
2 tbsp demerara sugar

1 Preheat the oven to 220°C/200°C fan/Gas 7 and line a baking sheet with baking paper.

2 Measure the nuts, caster sugar and almond extract into a bowl and mix together.

3 Lay the pastry on a lightly floured work surface and re-roll it out to a rectangle measuring about 27 x 35cm (11 x 14in). Brush the pastry with egg white, sprinkle over the nut mixture and then the demerara sugar.

4 Lay a piece of cling film on top, then roll over the cling film with a rolling pin to press the nuts into the pastry. Slice the pastry in half lengthways so you have two strips.

5 Slice each strip widthways into about 15 straws. Hold the bottom edge of one strip and turn it over twice, to form two twists in the pastry, and place on the prepared baking sheet. Repeat with the remaining straws. Brush with more egg white and bake in the oven for 12–15 minutes or until golden brown and crisp. Set aside on a wire rack to cool.

MULLED WINE

THE SMELL OF MULLED WINE ALONE is enough to make the home Christmassy. I love to have it simmering from Christmas Eve through to Boxing Day night! The Mincemeat and Orange Feathered Tarts (page 291) go particularly well with a glass.

....

SERVES 12

3 lemons
2 large oranges
12 cloves
2 satsumas or clementines
2 bottles of red wine
2 cinnamon sticks
150g caster sugar

1 Peel the zest very thinly from the lemons and 1 orange, and squeeze out the juice. Stick the cloves into the satsumas. Thinly slice the remaining orange and cut into small pieces and reserve for decoration.

2 Pour the wine, 1.2 litres (2 pints) of water, citrus peel and juices into a large pan, and add the clove-studded satsumas and the cinnamon sticks. Bring just to the boil then lower the heat, cover and simmer for about an hour. Stir in the sugar gradually, to taste.

3 Strain the wine and serve hot, with the reserved orange pieces floating on the top.

MINCEMEAT AND ORANGE FEATHERED TARTS

PERFECT FOR THE FESTIVE SEASON – grating marzipan on top of these tarts is quicker than topping with pastry and gives a wonderful flavour too.

....

MAKES 12 TARTS

PREPARE AHEAD
The tarts can be make up to 3 days ahead and stored in an airtight container.

FREEZE
The tarts can be frozen, well wrapped, for up to 2 months.

FOR THE PASTRY
175g (6oz) plain flour
75g (3oz) cold butter, cubed
25g (1oz) icing sugar, plus extra for
   dusting
grated zest of 1 large orange (see tip)
1 egg, beaten

FOR THE FILLING
250g (9oz) good-quality mincemeat
100g (4oz) ready-to-eat dried
   apricots, finely chopped
100g (4oz) natural marzipan, grated
   (see tip)

1 You will need a 12-hole bun tin and an 8cm (3in) fluted pastry cutter. Preheat the oven to 200°C/180°C fan/Gas 6 and place a baking sheet inside to heat up.

2 First make the pastry, either by mixing the flour and butter in a food processor or by hand – rubbing the flour and butter together with your fingertips, until the mixture resembles breadcrumbs. Add the icing sugar and orange zest and mix in briefly, then add the egg. Mix until the dough just holds together, then wrap in greaseproof paper and place in the fridge to chill for 15 minutes.

3 Roll the pastry out very thinly on a floured work surface, to 1–2mm (1/16in) thick (see tip). Stamp out 12 rounds with the pastry cutter and use these to line the bun tin. Prick the base of each pastry case with a fork.

4 To make the filling, mix the mincemeat with the chopped apricots and divide between the pastry cases. Top with the grated marzipan.

5 Slide the bun tin on to the hot baking sheet inside the oven and bake for 12–15 minutes until golden and crisp. Dust with icing sugar and serve warm.

TIPS
For a stronger orange flavour, you could add half the zest to the pastry and half to the filling.

Chill the marzipan in the fridge to make it easier to grate.

Wrap the pastry in greaseproof paper, then roll between two pieces of paper or cling film to make a thin layer that doesn't stick to the rolling pin. Any leftover pastry can be used to make jam tarts.

COOK'S NOTES

WEIGHING AND MEASURING

• When you're using the recipes in this book, you're welcome to make little tweaks of your own. For example, I use a modest amount of chilli so you may wish to increase the amount to your taste. While it's best to follow exact weights where these are given first time round, you could use a bit more or a bit less to suit your taste next time. Equally, you might prefer to substitute one type of cheese for another in a recipe or use a different kind of fish or meat. Feel free to experiment and ring the changes.

• Both metric and imperial measures are provided. When you're weighing out ingredients, it's best to go by one or the other – never mix the two. (See also the Conversion Tables on pages 296–7.)

• Spoon measures are level unless otherwise stated.

• In recipes for cakes and other baked items, the ingredients need to be measured carefully. I find that digital scales are best for the purpose.

• For oven temperatures, the standard Centigrade measure is given first, followed by the fan temperature, 20 degrees less in each case. (See also the Conversion Tables on pages 296–7.) As ovens vary in the amount of heat they produce, you may need to cook a dish for slightly more or less time, depending on your own particular oven. It can be helpful to use an oven thermometer to gauge the correct temperature for cooking a dish.

FREEZING AND DEFROSTING

• If a recipe has no 'Freeze' note, then this means it's not suitable for freezing.

• You can freeze a freshly cooked dish, but raw ingredients – especially meat and fish – that have been frozen already should never be frozen again from raw. If meat or fish is carefully thawed and cooked at once in casseroles, pies or fishcakes, then these can be frozen for up to a month.

• Label everything when you put it in to freeze, including the date when it was frozen. Keep track of what is in the freezer in a notebook, striking things off as you use them from the freezer.

• Allow dishes to cool down fully before freezing. Empty ice-cream and soup cartons, washed out properly and with tight-fitting lids, make ideal containers for freezing soft fruit, soup and casseroles. Otherwise food (such as a tart or cake) should be wrapped in cling film then foil, or wrapped in a strong freezer bag.

• Frozen dishes should be defrosted thoroughly, ideally overnight in the fridge, before being cooked through until piping hot. Take the dish out of the fridge an hour before cooking to allow it to come to room temperature. Once defrosted, it should be reheated only once.

INGREDIENTS

• Where a type of cooking oil isn't specified, you can use any oil that you like, although it's best to choose something relatively mild, such as sunflower oil, that won't overpower the flavour of the dish. For dressings, use the best-quality oil that you can afford, to give the most intense flavour.

• For pastry and cakes, I've often specified butter as it gives much the best flavour, but you can use baking spreads instead (indeed, I've sometimes suggested using a spread, rather than butter, for its lightness of texture) using the all-in-one bowl method. Just make sure that the spread you choose is intended for baking. If using butter for baking, I prefer unsalted. When using the creaming method of making cakes, use softened butter.

• Where a small quantity of sugar (a teaspoonful or less) is given in the ingredients for a dish, often the type isn't specified, which means that you can use any type you wish.

• I use granulated sugar for general sweetening; caster sugar, which is finer, for baking; and icing sugar for icing. Light muscovado gives a great flavour and demerara creates delicious crunchy toppings and adds a fudgy flavour to cakes and puddings. All these sugars keep for long periods in sealed containers. If you find after a time the sugar has become a solid block in the bag, store a clean, damp J-cloth in the bag to separate the grains.

• Modern milling techniques mean that it is not always necessary to sift flour – I always specify in a recipe where it is needed.

• To turn plain flour into self-raising flour, add 2–3 teaspoons of baking powder to every 200g (7oz) of plain flour. Check the sell-by dates on flour and baking powder as they do lose their potency over time.

• If size is relevant in a recipe (whether something is small, medium or large), then this is stated in the ingredients list. It is omitted otherwise.

• Eggs are large, unless otherwise stated, and I prefer free range, if possible.

• Because of the potential salmonella risk in eggs, it is recommended that recipes using raw eggs are avoided by young children, pregnant women and anyone in ill-health. However, eggs carrying the British Lion Quality stamp are pasteurised, which limits the risk of salmonella.

• If you find yourself with leftover egg yolks, for example after making meringues, they don't freeze as well as egg whites, so cover them with a little water and store them in a container in the fridge for 2–3 days. Use them for mayonnaise, custard or lemon curd.

• Try to buy the best-quality meat and fish that you can afford – free range, in the case of meat, and sustainably sourced fish. Check with you fishmonger, or at the fish counter in your local supermarket, and use an alternative type of fish if you find that the kind you have selected is no longer on the sustainability list – which changes according to fish stock levels.

• Fresh herbs, except basil, can be kept in the fridge in a jug, covered with a freezer bag, for up to a week.

• Fresh parsley can be curly- or flat-leafed.

STORE-CUPBOARD BASICS

The following are some of the basic items that I keep in my larder, fridge and freezer and turn to all the time when I'm cooking. While the specifics will vary from household to household, ensuring you have some of these ingredients in reserve will help you to whip up a recipe at a moment's notice.

Larder:

Plain and self-raising flour

Sugar (caster, demerara, fondant icing sugar, icing sugar, muscovado)

Cocoa powder

Plain chocolate (for baking)

Shelled nuts (chestnuts, hazelnuts, pecan nuts, walnuts)

Flaked almonds

Ground almonds

Dried fruits for cakes

Stock cubes

Ground spices (cardamom, cayenne pepper, Chinese five-spice, cinnamon, cloves, coriander, cumin, curry powder, mixed spice, paprika, turmeric)

Salt and peppercorns

Gravy browning

Soy sauce

Mustard (Dijon and grainy)

Worcestershire sauce

Honey

Golden syrup

White wine vinegar

Balsamic vinegar

Cooking oils (olive, sunflower)

Tinned tomatoes

Tinned black-eyed beans

Passata

Tomato purée

Lentils (Puy, red)

Short- and long-grain rice

Pasta in different shapes and sizes

Fridge:

Milk

Cream

Butter

Baking spread

Cheeses (mature Cheddar, Parmesan, Stilton)

Eggs

Mayonnaise

Horseradish sauce

Redcurrant jelly

Salad ingredients (cucumber, fresh tomatoes, salad leaves)

Freezer:

Home-grown vegetables and fruit (including soft fruit for making puddings and coulis)

Shop-bought peas and small broad beans

Milk

Bread

Dough balls

Sausages

Chicken breasts

Smoked trout and salmon

Homemade chicken stock

Ice cream

Packets of puff pastry

Homemade dishes (casseroles, lasagne, meatballs, minced beef)

Fresh root ginger

SERVING QUANTITIES

When you're cooking a meal for a gathering, large or small, it's very easy to overestimate what you'll need, with the result that you end up cooking too much and with a lot of leftovers that can be difficult to store. I've therefore included a rough quantities calculator below that you may find helpful when planning a meal. Quantities will vary, of course, depending on your guests (especially if they include hungry teenagers!), the time of day/year and the type of meal you have in mind.

Savoury dishes, per person:

Joint with bone: 175–225g (6–8oz)

Joint without bone: 100–175g (4–6oz)

Meat for casseroles: 175g (6oz)

Steak: 175g (6oz)

Pasta, uncooked: 75–100g (3–4oz)

Rice, uncooked: 40–50g (1½–2oz)

Fish: 100–125g (4–4½oz)

Soup: 600ml (1 pint) will serve 3 people

Sweet dishes, per person:

Cakes: a 20cm (8in) sandwich sponge will serve 8

Meringues: 1 egg white and 50g (2oz) caster sugar will make about 5 small meringues

Soft fruits: 75–100g (3–4oz)

Cream to accompany desserts: 600ml (1 pint) per 12 portions

Milk for tea: 600ml (1 pint) per 20 cups

Conversion tables

Measurements

METRIC	IMPERIAL
5mm	¼in
1cm	½in
2.5cm	1in
5cm	2in
7.5cm	3in
10cm	4in
12.5cm	5in
15cm	6in
18cm	7in
20cm	8in
23cm	9in
25cm	10in
30cm	12in

Oven temperatures

°C	FAN °C	°F	GAS MARK
140°C	Fan 120°C	275°F	Gas 1
150°C	Fan 130°C	300°F	Gas 2
160°C	Fan 140°C	325°F	Gas 3
180°C	Fan 160°C	350°F	Gas 4
190°C	Fan 170°C	375°F	Gas 5
200°C	Fan 180°C	400°F	Gas 6
220°C	Fan 200°C	425°F	Gas 7
230°C	Fan 210°C	450°F	Gas 8
240°C	Fan 220°C	475°F	Gas 9

VOLUME

METRIC	IMPERIAL
25ml	1fl oz
50ml	2fl oz
85ml	3fl oz
100ml	3½fl oz
150ml	5fl oz (¼ pint)
200ml	7fl oz
300ml	10fl oz (½ pint)
450ml	15fl oz (¾ pint)
600ml	1 pint
700ml	1¼ pints
900ml	1½ pints
1 litre	1¾ pints
1.2 litres	2 pints
1.25 litres	2¼ pints
1.5 litres	2½ pints
1.6 litres	2¾ pints
1.75 litres	3 pints
1.8 litres	3¼ pints
2 litres	3½ pints
2.1 litres	3¾ pints
2.25 litres	4 pints
2.75 litres	5 pints
3.4 litres	6 pints
3.9 litres	7 pints
4.5 litres	8 pints (1 gallon)

WEIGHTS

METRIC	IMPERIAL
15g	½oz
25g	1oz
40g	1½oz
50g	2oz
75g	3oz
100g	4oz
150g	5oz
175g	6oz
200g	7oz
225g	8oz
250g	9oz
275g	10oz
350g	12oz
375g	13oz
400g	14oz
425g	15oz
450g	1lb
550g	1¼lb
675g	1½lb
750g	1¾lb
900g	2lb
1.5kg	3lb
1.75kg	4lb
2.25kg	5lb

INDEX

Note: page numbers in **bold** refer to photographs.

THANK YOUS

IT HAS BEEN A SHEER DELIGHT to write this book to accompany my BBC TV series.

I am always grateful to Lucy Young who has now been with me for a quarter of a century!! Her unfaltering enthusiasm for perfection with all the recipes is second to none, and Luc even enjoys checking the proofs (something I am less keen on!). We test all the recipes to perfection – thanks to Lucinda McCord and Angela Patel for their months in the kitchen, giving attention to every detail to make sure every recipe is foolproof. The book was completed before we filmed the series, so that we could add even more tips and hints at that stage, too. Family and friends seem to have insatiable appetites and are devoted tasters.

A big thank you, too, to Lizzy Gray and Kate Fox at Ebury for being such a brilliant editing team and a delight to work with. Georgia Glynn Smith is a genius photographer, not only for the food shots but she followed me around the country capturing the most interesting moments which make this book so special. Our home economists Lisa Harrison and Georgia May who are heaven to work with and put their heart and soul into everything they do. Plus the rest of the team: Liz Belton, Lucy Gowans, Lizzie Kamenetzky and Kate Parker. Finally, to Fiona Lindsay at Limelight Management for her sound advice.

How lucky I am to be with working with such a great team!